CONDITIONAL BELONGING

Conditional Belonging

*The Racialization of Iranians in the
Wake of Anti-Muslim Politics*

Sahar Sadeghi

NEW YORK UNIVERSITY PRESS
New York

NEW YORK UNIVERSITY PRESS
New York
www.nyupress.org

Please contact the Library of Congress for Cataloging-in-Publication data.
ISBN: 9781479804993 (hardback)
ISBN: 9781479805013 (paperback)
ISBN: 9781479805037 (library ebook)
ISBN: 9781479805020 (consumer ebook)

New York University Press books are printed on acid-free paper, and their binding materials are chosen for strength and durability. We strive to use environmentally responsible suppliers and materials to the greatest extent possible in publishing our books.

Manufactured in the United States of America

10 9 8 7 6 5 4 3 2 1

Also available as an ebook

To my parents, for all their sacrifices

This is how sweet and free of fear I feel now in myself. Beyond opinion and judgment, undistracted by guilt, I am walking steadily home, not timid, or uncertain, with my eyes splendidly clear, all one pearl of gratefulness, no fear.

—"Mowlana" Rumi

CONTENTS

Introduction

My recollection of the first five years of my life is growing up in a loving family. We lived practically next door to my grandparents, and I would see them almost daily. My aunts, uncles, and countless cousins also surrounded me, and gathering at my uncle Ali's house on Fridays was the norm. I had no idea there was a war going on because we lived in Tehran and were mostly protected from the traumatic realities of the Iran-Iraq war.

Most of my family did not leave Iran before the revolution. Then in the mid-1980s, amid the Iran-Iraq war, most of my extended family, one family followed by another, left. I have never asked my parents why we waited so long, why we did not leave at the onset of the revolution like so many others, but I think I know the answer to that question. My parents, like many others, were waiting to see how the revolution progressed and whether the new government would fulfill its promises. It did not. As a result, my uncles went to Canada; several cousins went to the Netherlands; and an aunt, cousins, and my parents and I went to Germany. Then in the early 1990s my parents and I became twice migrants by immigrating to northern California.

Twenty-seven years later I was immersed in my dissertation fieldwork on the Iranian diaspora. Conducting that research coupled with my own layered experiences with migration and Iran made me long for Iran and family even more. Iran was constantly on my mind, yet I had not been there since I was a child. I felt this intense longing to visit. In 2011, I got the opportunity to go back. I had heard mostly good things about visiting from Iranian friends and acquaintances, as well as my interlocutors, and had no real reservations or worries. Of course, there were a few family members living outside Iran who felt anxious and thought there might be some risk in going, but what Iranian doesn't have a few relatives who are adamant about not visiting Iran?

My mother and I flew from San Francisco to Tehran in the summer of 2011. I had finally returned after being gone for twenty-seven years. I felt the vibrations there and remembered them. It was during these trips that I also got to know my grandmother and larger family more intimately. My grandfather had passed four years prior, and it had greatly saddened me that I could not attend his funeral. Now that I had made my way back to Iran, I wanted to make up for all the years I felt I had lost. The circumstances of the migration of Iranians had been hard and traumatizing both for those who had felt compelled to leave and those who stayed behind. I had questions for my grandmother—I wanted to hear her thoughts about our migration and the migration of so many others out of Iran after the revolution.

I returned in 2014. This time I also visited my father's childhood city of Arak and spent time with my *Ame* (my father's sister). With my mother and grandmother, I also went to Tafresh, the city where my maternal and paternal grandparents were born and raised before they migrated to Tehran and Arak. Tafresh is known for its massive gardens (*bagh*) and farms. I visited my grandparents' *bagh* and saw the fruit trees my grandfather had planted prior to his passing. I felt deeply connected to my family history while I was there and felt the importance and gravity of my being there. I also visited the holy city of Mashhad, paid my respects at the Imam Reza shrine, and shopped at the grand bazaar for Firuze jewelry. I even got to see the city of Shiraz, visited the Tomb of Hafez and the beautiful gardens, and ate the most delicious *faloodeh shirazi*. Every trip made me fall in love with Iran and its people even more, and while it had been a few decades since we migrated, I did not feel like an outsider there but rather as someone who had taken a long time to get back home.

My third trip took place after finishing research in Germany in the summer of 2016. I was going to spend six days with my grandmother, just me and her. The flight to Tehran only took four hours, and I remember lamenting how easily I could visit my family in Iran if we still lived in Germany. "How lucky are Iranians in Europe to be so close," is something I remember saying to myself in an envious tone. I also realize now that this trip was particularly special to me because it was my first solo trip to Iran. I had come and gone with ease and my explorations had just started. I would be back next summer.

Sadly, the election of Donald Trump changed many things. The passing of the Muslim Ban in the early part of 2017 had enflamed Iran-US political relations and made travel to and from Iran precarious. Given my background as an academic who studies the Iranian diaspora, I was persistently discouraged from going to Iran until "he is out of office." Three years had gone by, and I had not seen my grandmother, so in early 2020 I decided that politics would no longer stand in my way, and I would visit my grandmother that summer. Then COVID-19 happened, and borders closed, and travel came to a halt. Time waits for no one, and before I could go back and see her, my grandmother, Akram Sadeghi, transitioned in August 2020. She was my last living grandparent, and our relationship has always felt interrupted because of the uncertain political alliances and relations between the nations that we resided in. The years lost between seeing each other are a sore reminder of the very real ways that politics impact even the most intimate aspects of our lives.

Unlike other immigrants able to be transnational and see family frequently—even spending summers together—I never had those opportunities or experiences because the severing of US-Iran relations drastically changed travel from and to Iran. For instance, there is no US embassy in Iran and no Iranian embassy in the US, tourist visas to the US are difficult to attain, and Iranians must travel to Turkey or other nearby countries to apply for one. This means that many Iranians, especially those living in the US, go years before reuniting with family in Iran—sometimes only seeing each other once or twice in a decade. Many precious years are lost in the shuffle. I saw my grandparents seldom, and I would not reunite with my aunts and uncles and cousins until many years later.

My story emphasizes how the migration of Iranians has been inextricably shaped by political affairs and policy and to underscore that the factors and conditions that spurred the migration of so many Iranians were political. Many of our families left and did not know how long the Iranian Revolution would last or whether the newly established government would remain. A lot of decisions were made on a whim, because, for most, the plan was to return when things calmed down. My family migrated to Germany, a nation with a universal asylum policy where they had existing networks and ties. Like the Iranians who participated in this research, I have family scattered throughout the world, and this dispersal means that there are family members and elders whom I love but with whom my time has been cut short because seeing each other is difficult. Although this research is larger in scope, being a twice migrant who has lived in two different nations with varying attributes and identities has influenced this project in significant ways. Being an Iranian child in Germany and then an adolescent and young adult in California has served as the foundation of my interests in this comparative research. It has driven my curiosities about how the environments that we live in influence our relationships to those given spaces.

My migration history has also taught me valuable lessons about race and racism. The drastic shift of moving to a predominately white middle-class city and neighborhood in the United States as an adolescent also showed me a few things—for example, that Americans really disliked Arabs (even more than Iranians did) and that Americans thought Iraq and Iran were the same country. Given that I had migrated from Germany, some may be surprised to hear that it was northern California that introduced me to explicit Islamophobia and anti–Middle Eastern racism. How could I have moved from Germany—a nation often seen as the bastion of racism—to a place regarded as the "land of immigrants and opportunity" and be treated with such hostility? Little did I know then that the way each nation "did race" was not necessarily the same. We migrated in 1992, a year after the Gulf War ended, a time when anti-Arab and anti–Middle Eastern prejudice and racism was particularly

pronounced. We had also migrated to a nation that had a history of seeing Iranians and those "from that part of the world" as foreign enemies
and terrorists, especially since the Iranian Revolution and the hostage
crisis of the early 1980s. The terrorist attacks of 9/11 ignited another cycle
of bigotry in the United States. My personal experiences—especially
those of exclusion—have deeply influenced the way I understand experiences of racialization and belonging and helped me distinguish the
similarities and differences between being a foreigner in Germany and
being Iranian, Middle Eastern, and Muslim in the US.

As I show, Iranians are racialized in both nations, albeit in different ways, and this has much to do with how each nation has used race,
descent, and culture as criteria for citizenship and national membership. Specifically, the book provides a comparative analysis of racialization processes among Iranians in two national contexts—the US and
Germany—that have different credos and national narratives. America,
it is often believed, is a "color-blind" nation made up of immigrants,
and Germany is thought to be a refugee-accepting society, even if it
lacks extensive immigration policy. In the US, the race-based dimensions of both immigration and citizenship are more hidden than in
Germany, which creates the illusion of inclusivity and equality. In Germany, race- or blood-based citizenship was not eliminated until 2000,
and for decades second- and third-generation children of migrants (the
most explicit case being the Turks) were virtually excluded from having
equal civil rights.[1] Unlike Germany, though, as I elaborate in chapter 3,
the racialization of Iranians in the US is more clearly dependent on the
severing of US-Iran ties after the revolution and hostage crisis, and on
larger foreign policy and racial projects in the Middle East, than them
being immigrants or foreigners. In Germany, racialization is less about
Iranian-German relations and foreign policy and more tied to lingering
German nationalism and anti-foreigner sentiment and racism.

Importantly, in both contexts, the racialization of Iranians is a part
of larger racial projects that have constructed and deemed "foreigners,"
Ausländers, "immigrants," Muslims, and people from the Middle East

as "others." Racial projects, as defined by Omi and Winant (1986), are "simultaneously an interpretation, representation, or explanation of racial identities and meanings, and an effort to organize and distribute resources along particular racial lines" (p. 125). Racial projects create the category of a racial other and a political-economic system in which material conditions and resources for the "other" are organized. Cainkar and Selod (2018) consider the specific political interests and objectives that racial projects serve; they argue that "Muslims, Arabs, and South Asians have been racialized by the same racial project that ideologically deploys an essentialized narrative of 'terror threat' working in tandem with state and civil society" (p. 165). Racial projects, like the "war on terror," and geopolitical conflict and the continuation of colonial projects in the greater South West Asian and North African (SWANA) region require a set of racial ideologies that describe, categorize, and create a commonsense understanding of what makes the "other" different.

The book also explores the place of Iranians in the context of critical international events. It reveals how global politics, diplomatic relations, and asylum and immigration policy have impacted various facets of life, including the decisions Iranians have made about settlement and migration, attempts at integration, race/ethnic identification, racialization, and the extent to which they belong and possess social membership. Considering geopolitical arrangements means taking the role of foreign policy into account, including economic relations and foreign investment between Iran and the US, and Iran and Germany historically and currently. Some examples of critical international events and policies that have influenced how Iranians have been racialized and politicized include the Iranian Revolution of 1979, the 1980 hostage crisis, the Iranian uranium enrichment program, the 2015 refugee crisis, the 2016 Iran Deal, the 2017 travel ban executive order (the so-called Muslim Ban), and the Trump administration's decertification of the 2016 Iran Deal and reimposition of economic sanctions on Iran. Importantly, the racialization of Iranians changes and shifts according to political context and larger global political events.

The book draws on two waves of qualitative fieldwork and longitudinal interviews with eighty-eight Iranians, first- and second-generation Iranians living in northern and southern California and Hamburg, Germany. The interviews demonstrate how racialization and racism fluctuate, shift, and transform according to political events and context. The follow-up interviews conducted after the 2015 global refugee crisis in Europe and the 2016 Trump presidential election are especially illustrative. They show how heightened racial and religious stigma and marginality among first- and second-generation Iranians in Germany and the US is significantly tied to the rise of right-leaning populist political parties and movements—and explicitly anti-migrant and anti-Muslim policies. Racial and social boundaries have seemingly hardened,[2] and the dividing line of "who belongs" and "who does not belong" has become more pronounced and salient along race, culture, and religion. This has helped promote increased feelings of "perpetual foreignness" for Iranians in Germany, and experiences of racialization, Islamophobia, anti-Muslim discrimination, and violence in the US. Iranian immigrants and their children have responded to this marginalization and racialization by developing strategies for coping with and maneuvering around the exclusion and racism. The notions of *racial flexibility* and *cultural flexibility* describe how conceptions of citizenship, race, and belonging determine what strategies are available to the people I spoke with for coping with the exclusion and racism they encountered.[3]

Importantly, this research speaks to past and more recent scholarship on Iranians in diaspora.[4] This book makes two specific contributions to this growing body of knowledge. First, the comparative aspects of this research provide a unique opportunity to tease out the attributes, factors, and policies that shape the lives of Iranians and that are similar and different among the experiences of Iranians in diaspora. For example, past research has shown how European states, like Germany, that offer more expansive social-welfare benefits also maintain barriers to social mobility for immigrants and their children,[5] whereas in the

US the welfare state is limited but upward mobility through credentials and education—one's human capital—is more feasible. And second, this book advances our understanding of the role and power of global politics and foreign policy in shaping racial and political stigmatization. Much of the scholarship on the Iranian diaspora has focused on the experiences of first-generation Iranians in the US and dealt with the themes of integration and mobility. This research generally described Iranians as high-skilled immigrants who have attained high educational credentials, or become entrepreneurs, which enabled a significant portion of the Iranian community to become middle-class and have middle-class experiences in the US. The literature about Iranians in Europe is also mostly centered on the experiences of the first generation and is focused on Iranians' inclinations toward self-employment, their experiences of employment discrimination, migration, and subsequent changes to Iranian family structures, as well as political activism.[6] This body of scholarship provided an important intellectual foundation and offered glimpses into the lives of post-revolution Iranian immigrants and refugees in the US, Canada, and Europe. More recent scholarship on the Iranian diaspora is increasingly focused on the lives and identities of second-generation Iranians, race and identity, citizenship and belonging, and foreign policy, specifically Iran-US political relations. I consider this book to be a part of this growing field of Iranian diaspora studies and hope that it advances our knowledge about how global and local politics influence self-identification, racialization, and social belonging.

Racial States, National Narratives, and Citizenship

The explanatory agenda of this book, and the development of a more precise elaboration of racialization in the context of global politics, grows from an extended conversation with Orientalism, racial formation theory, critical race theory, and boundary theory. More specifically, the centrality of race and culture in national identity and social membership, immigration policy, and citizenship is examined through an engagement with scholarship on nation-state making and nationalism. Nations are constructed, and stories are told of how they came to exist. National identity contains a set of ideas, beliefs, and myths that shape who is a member of a national community—an "imagined community"[7]—and is granted access to social citizenship. These narratives manifest themselves politically in state constitutions, immigration laws, and laws concerning civil rights. Western societies have typically relied upon phenotypically distinguishable traits—especially skin color—to decide who is included in the polity, or nation, and who is excluded.[8] The nation and its member—the imagined collectivity—are conceptualized as being united by blood or descent. Throughout the modern era, European nations and the United States have persistently employed race/ethnic-based nationalism to exclude non-European and other undesirable groups or populations from having social, civic, and political rights. These rights included the ability to be citizens or have the same rights that other citizens had.[9] Given that Western liberal states have historically functioned as racial states, the very notion of liberalism is indeed a racialized (white) liberalism where whiteness is a prerequisite for the attainment of individualism, equal rights, citizenship, and moral equality.[10] According to Fredrickson (2002), when differences that may otherwise be described as ethno-cultural become regarded as innate, natural, and unchangeable then racist beliefs/ideologies are said to exist. Historically, both the US and Germany have had "overtly racist regimes" that utilized theories and practices like social Darwinism and eugenics to legitimize genocide, enslavement, overseas colonization, and the Holocaust.[11]

The Centrality of Race vs. the Myth of Immigrant America

The myth of immigrant America is the dominant framework used to describe American sentiments toward immigrants.[12] According to Kohn (1957), the idea of the "United States as a land with open gateways, a nation of many nations, became as important for American nationalism as its identification with the idea of individual liberty and its federal character (p. 26)." Behdad (2005) argues that "the notion of cultural and political assimilation has always accompanied the myth of immigrant America" and that newcomers must "lose their old national 'skins' to become American citizens" (p. 31). According to some, immigrants are seen as having successfully become American when they culturally and politically assimilate to national identity, character, and values.

The idea of the US as a liberal state, one that is "immigrant receiving," in which everyone is treated equally is challenged and contradicted by the centrality of race and racism historically and in contemporary US society. The United States is a nation born out of the enslavement of Africans and the genocide of indigenous tribes and native peoples. Its economic wealth and prosperity were rooted in the labor of enslaved people and the conquering of native lands. Industrialization and economic development also relied upon the exploitation of Mexican laborers in the southwest, Chinese immigrants, eastern European Jews, and other southern and eastern Europeans. Racial oppression and subjugation and waves of immigration have created the multiracial and ethnic composition of the US.[13] Yet still, race was a main criterion in citizenship policy, and access to citizenship determined the ability to vote and own land. Immigrants from Europe—especially western and northern Europe—were preferred for citizenship compared to Chinese, South Asian, and Japanese immigrants. Being legally classified as "white" is how entry to citizenship, property, and civil rights was gained, and who could have access to this "whiteness" was fervently debated throughout the early 1900s.

Supreme Court decisions from the early 1920s highlight the racial construction of US citizenship. For example, various Asian groups, including Japanese, Filipinos, and those who were Hindu, were considered "nonwhite and hence ineligible of citizenship."[14] US courts determined eligibility for citizenship based on whether groups were "white" in the eyes of the law, and this qualification was arbitrary and not fixed.[15] During the era of restrictive naturalization, immigrants who fell into the category of "not quite white" used various mechanisms to petition the state to prove their "whiteness" to the court. The history of Syrian and Lebanese immigrants, for example, provides ample evidence of how racial classifications shift and the consequences of such changes.[16] Up until the early 1900s Syrians were considered white, but the rise of nativism, racist ideology, and restrictions on foreign-born immigrants pushed Syrians and Lebanese out of the white racial category. In 1914, the decision in *Dow v. United States* declared that Syrians and Lebanese—and by default other Middle Eastern groups—were officially "white" and eligible for naturalization. Most of these immigrants were Christian,[17] which undoubtedly played a role in the perception of the courts that they were indeed white.

In 1952, naturalization restrictions were finally lifted for non-white immigrants, and they became eligible for citizenship regardless of their national origins. As a result of these changes, immigrants who have attained permanent residency can become naturalized citizens, and those who are born on US soil are citizens.[18] As with citizenship, prior to 1965, US immigration policies were also exclusionary. In 1924, Congress established race-based national-origins quotas with the intent to curtail immigration from the "less desirable" nations of southern and eastern Europe and Asia and increase immigration from northern and western Europe. Although restrictive immigration policies were modified in 1952, an unbiased immigration policy was not established in the US until 1965. Furthermore, citizenship and immigration policies during the early twentieth century reinforced one another; race-based criteria were utilized in the formation of both immigration policies and naturalization laws. The "imagined community" has been overwhelmingly informed by race and national origins. Despite this history, though, the "nation of immigrants" narrative remains powerful. It continues to create the illusion that it has always been open and welcoming to new migrants, regardless of their racial/ethnic, national origins, and religious backgrounds.

The current main ideological framework of America being a "color-blind" society, or a nation of immigrants with open opportunity structures, denies the salience of race and systemic racism.[19] It also does not acknowledge how race continues to inform all aspects of American life—from laws, culture, media, and policies to economics and wealth. Racialized social structures and the social, political, and ideological practices that produce differential status between racial groups and institutional forms of racism have remained even after the Civil Rights Movement and laws passed to officially eliminate racial segregation and racism.[20] Living in a society that espouses "color-blindness" means that the persistence of racism is persistently explained away by providing nonracial rationales.[21]

Immigrants continue to migrate to the US in the hopes of attaining a better life, and most are not aware that they will inherit the histories and racial systems of their "new nation" and will also have to find their "place" in the racial order of things. The current racial stratification order in the US allows some racially ambiguous groups, or those who sit "at the margins of whiteness," to occupy "honorary white" status and achieve economic and educational mobility.[22] According to Bonilla-Silva (2004), the US is shifting from a biracial to a triracial stratification order like that of many Latin American countries. In this order, there is some flexibility for racially ambiguous groups, like Iranians, to pass as and be honorary whites. Maghbouleh's (2017) research on Iranians in the US highlights how Iranian Americans can approximate whiteness, but how they also sit at the limits of it.

From the Volk to Refugee-Receiving Society

Germany does not possess a dominant ideology of "color blindness" or of being an "immigrant-receiving nation." From the late seventeenth century—and especially the nineteenth onward—the ideas and frameworks of European Enlightenment and German Romanticism influenced German state making. The nation was regarded as "an extended family with one national character" and nationality as something that grows "naturally" from peculiar habits, customs, and traditions, which give "expression to the authentic folk spirit, *Volkgeist*."[23] Descent-based criteria were used to craft German[24] citizenship policy to exclude racially and socially "undesirable" people from having the same social, civic, and political rights.[25] "Blood" or ancestry, common language, shared culture and heritage, and religion were all used to produce a collective feeling of national unification.[26] An important component of the construction of German-ness was the inseparable link between race and nation. The "politics of citizenship . . . are politics of national interest,"[27] and the construction of citizenship is crucial to the nation-building process. Citizenship is meant to be internally inclusive and externally exclusive, and the institution of citizenship produces closure against non-members.

This descent-based conception of citizenship became national law in 1913 through the Nationality Law of the German Empire.[28] The German state justified its genocidal treatment of Jews and other socially marginalized groups by citing "irrefutable" racial, ethnic, religious, and cultural differences.[29] Nazism required deep-rooted theories and ideas about Aryan superiority and "biologic"[30] and immutable human differences. Nazism was defeated in 1945, and Germany's reentry into the international community was based on several stipulations. One was that asylum policy had to be codified into German basic law via article 16a. Asylum policy stated that "no state has the right to persecute an individual for his or her political or religious beliefs or other personal characteristics that mark him or her as different"[31] and that anyone experiencing political persecution[32] could apply for asylum. In 1951, Germany became a participant in the Geneva Convention Relating to the Status of Refugees, and official refugee policy was incorporated into section 3 of the German Asylum Act.[33] Thus, after the fall of Nazism at the end of World War II, Germany became a liberal state—with a socially democratic government and a mandate to accept refugees and asylum seekers. This ushered in an era of German socialism and humanitarian policies, yet remnants of racial nationalism remained in German law and policy. For example, the ancestry criteria in citizenship law remained long after the collapse of the Third Reich and was not removed until decades later. And it was only at the beginning of the twenty-first century, on January 1, 2000, that the social and political rights of non-German immigrants and their children—including a significant number of second- and third-generation Turks—were expanded.

In contemporary German society, racialized conceptions of German nationhood and national identity and the continuing importance of Christianity and German cultural values[34] are obscured through the language of liberalism.[35] Full membership and equal participation in Germany—culturally, socially, and structurally—remains mostly accessible to individuals of German descent, and access to formal citizenship cannot erase the continuing significance and importance of race and ancestry in the crafting of state policy.[36] This presents a number of issues and contradictions for a seemingly humanitarian, refugee-accepting society that provides ample social welfare programs for foreigners and refugees, yet also harbors anti-foreigner sentiment and is seeing the rising popularity of right-wing political movements. The explicit ethno-racial conception of citizenship and belonging that long excluded populations, and justified the Holocaust, is not necessarily a relic of the past. And while we see a dominant narrative of equal human rights and democracy in the post–World War II and post–Civil Rights era, Bonilla-Silva and Mayorga (2011) remind us that "access to formal citizenship" does not disrupt the "racial order of things." For as long as nation-states remain "racial states" then "judicial-political categories such as citizenship will not confer full equality."[37]

Orientalism and Racialization

What does it mean to exist and live in nations with a racial past and racialized social systems? What factors have contributed to and made the racialization of Iranians possible? How is this racial othering related to existing racial projects? How is belonging possible and attainable if social membership and social citizenship is race-based? Iranians in the

US are legally classified as white, but their everyday experiences do not necessarily reflect this. In both the US and Germany, when Iranians are "racialized" and "racially othered" a number of racial meanings and specific set of physical and cultural differences are externally ascribed onto them.[38] For example, terms such as "hostage takers," "terrorist-sponsoring," "Axis of Evil," *Ausländer* (foreigner), and *Schwarzkopf* (a slur suggesting someone is a dark-haired foreigner) label an entire group and culture of people as "others."

I use Said's framework of Orientalism to help link the racialization of Iranians to larger colonial discourses and the systems of ideologies that produced the category of an "other." Orientalism is an ideological apparatus by which the West has constructed and defined the "Orient" and "Middle East and Near East." The term "Middle East," for example, is not a term or category subjectively crafted by the people of those regions, rather it is a geopolitical concept, externally crafted and imposed upon the people of a diverse set of cultures and nations.[39] Said (1978) explains that this imaginary ideal of the Orient creates falsely unifying categories such as "Muslim," "America," "the East," and "the West." Relatedly, Goldberg's (2008) analysis of nineteenth-century depictions of Muslims "as the quintessential outsider . . . strange in ways, habits, and ability to self-govern, aggressive, emotional, and conniving" is critical. The construction of the Muslim and blackness went hand in hand— Arabs were seen as being "barely above Africans," especially Moors and North Africans.[40]

The categorization of numerous regions, people, and cultures into one collective is an effective mechanism to define groups monolithically. This lumping makes it easier to colonize, wage war, and dominate, because these populations are seen as "all the same." The construction of the Iranian people as "hostage takers" or "terrorist-sponsoring" and the vilification and racialization of Middle Easterners, Muslims, and Muslim-identified immigrants as terrorists have been commonplace and persistent since the 1967 Arab-Israeli war, the Iranian Revolution and hostage crisis, the Gulf War, and 9/11. Cainkar (2009) argues that the discriminatory and negative treatment of Arabs and Muslims in the US did not start with 9/11 but was rather caused by "pre-existing conditions that configured people who would readily conduct and approve of such attacks" (p. 2). In the post-9/11 era, the racialization of Middle Easterners and Muslims is inextricably tied to foreign policy and the "war on terror."[41] According to Tehranian (2009), the "reproblematization of the Middle Eastern population from friendly foreigner to enemy alien, from enemy alien to enemy race is a trend that has been accelerated by the events of 9/11" (p. 7). The construction of Middle Easterners as "foreign enemies" and the widespread use of racial profiling and the violation of their civil rights are directly connected to state policies, such as Special Registration and the US Patriot Act.

Theoretical Contributions

Conditional Belonging

Throughout the following chapters, I will demonstrate how racialization and politicization facilitate experiences of social marginality, which ultimately impact social membership and belonging. I use the concepts of "being" and "belonging," articulated in the work of Levitt and Schiller (2004) to assess Iranians' experiences with social and racial citizenship. "Being" is defined as a state of existence that involves engagement in the social relations and practices of a given environment without one's identities belonging to that space. This means that individuals can be entrenched in and take part in institutions, organizations, experiences, and cultural practices on various levels, yet not identify with, or "belong" to, them. Belonging is relational and involves both conscious connection and identification.[42] It is not merely about individuals sharing a culture but requires the right to participate in the development of a living tradition.[43] Belonging is also tied to social citizenship, the feeling of being a member of the community, including "recognition by other members of the community."[44]

I argue that racialization and racial "othering" strips a person from being identified and recognized as a social member, a social citizen of a nation, despite having access to formal citizenship. This leads to something I call *conditional belonging*. As the stories of the Iranian interlocutors will show, citizenship does not guarantee social membership. I consider "conditional belonging" as Iranians partaking in the cultures, norms, practices, and state institutions of their host society, but not feeling like full, unconditional social membership is attainable. Not having full social membership has material effects such as political disenfranchisement and barriers to economic and social mobility, and it creates a sense of not being seen or treated like a full member of the larger society. This "conditional belonging" is often related to being racially othered and racialized. Examples of this lack of social membership, lack of belonging, and othering are also found in the work of Tuan (1998). The concept of "forever foreigner" illustrates this feeling and experience of being a stranger, a perpetual guest, or being perpetually foreign despite having lived in a nation for decades or generations. Being "perpetually foreign" is about being "from somewhere else." Being asked "where are you from" or "where are you really from" signals this sort of racialization and sense of perpetual foreignness. In the case of Iranians, it often the interplay between critical international events and global political policy, and national social and political climates, that influences the extent to which they feel themselves to be a member of the nations that they live in. Moreover, to ameliorate feelings of partial citizenship, of lack of social citizenship, Iranians employ several coping mechanisms aimed at maneuvering being racialized and marginalized. This ability to navigate is rooted in something I characterize as *racial flexibility* and *cultural flexibility*, and it is centrally tied to how each place "does race."

Racial and Cultural Flexibility

As I demonstrate in chapter 4, and as I have mentioned, Iranians aim to mediate, and cope with, the marginality and racism they experience through something I call *racial flexibility* in the US and *cultural flexibility* in Germany. This flexibility is based on each nation's racial boundaries and stratification system. I regard racial flexibility as the ability to bend, shift, and shape how one is racially/ethnically perceived through several *conscious* and *deliberate decisions*. The American racial stratification system allows Iranians, at times, to blend into whiteness, assuming a sort of "honorary white" position, like that proposed by Bonilla-Silva. The racial flexibility of Iranians is also situational, and more easily done in parts of the US where Iranians are in community with other racially ambiguous people, like light-skinned Latinos, Asian Indians, East Asians, and other Middle Easterners, compared to regions of the country where an explicitly Black-white racial boundary dominates. For example, Iranians are more likely to be able to attain "honorary white" status in places like the Bay Area or Los Angeles than in certain parts of California that are predominately white with no significant immigrant or minority populations.

Nations, like Germany, that maintain race-based and cultural definitions of national identity, nationality, and imagined community are unable to allow Iranians this kind of racial ambiguity and passing. Racial flexibility is not available to them; they have access to cultural flexibility, "which involves a set of gestures meant to signal and express cultural proximity to Germans," that they are "a familiar people" and not strangers. Iranians are not racially white in Germany and those whom I spoke with expressed in detail how ancestry-based definitions of social membership continue to dominate throughout German society. The rigidness of the social racial boundaries means that Iranians cannot pass into becoming German, and there is no other racial category they can pass into that would significantly reduce their marginality or identification as foreigners. At best, they can be culturally malleable, exhibit "cultural flexibility," and ultimately take up the category of "good foreigners." Being "good foreigners" is a response to racialization and also a coping mechanism, a means by which Iranians attempt to distance themselves from the "bad foreigners" and all of that category's negative connotations. This is a matter I take up in chapter 4 in greater detail when I analyze the responses and coping mechanisms that Iranians have adopted to deal with and overcome marginality.

Organization of the Book and Arguments

This book is composed of four data-based chapters and a conclusion, each dealing with major themes of Iranians' lived experiences in the US and Germany. Chapter 1 begins by examining the factors that facilitated the migration of Iranians to the US and Germany prior to the revolution of 1979 and then turns to migration in the post-revolution period. I point to significant differences related to diplomatic relations and foreign policy and asylum and refugee policy as shaping the varying settlement experiences of Iranians in each nation in the post-revolutionary period.

Chapter 2 examines the political relationship of the US and Iran over the last forty years and argues that the severing of diplomatic ties between the nations has had a profound impact on the treatment of Iranian immigrants in Western nations, specifically the US. This chapter considers how these dynamics have racialized and politicized Iranian communities in the US. I include follow-up interviews from 2017–2018 to show how the presidency of Donald Trump, the 2017 travel ban executive order (aka "the Muslim Ban"), and the decertification of the 2016 Iran Deal have heightened and renewed Iranians' fears and experiences of race and religious-based discrimination. I conclude this chapter with a discussion of the implications that policies which persistently associate Iranians with terrorism have for identity, citizenship, and belonging.

Chapter 3 considers how Germany's longer history of race-based citizenship and anti-foreigner racism influences how migrants and foreigners are perceived, discussed, and treated. It highlights how the racialized nature of German citizenship policy and contemporary state refugee policy influences current integration discourse and policy. It also examines Iranians' position as "good foreigners" in Germany to illustrate existing racial/ethnic boundaries, differentiation, and hierarchies and to underscore the limitations of cultural competence, citizenship, and economic mobility in ameliorating marginality and discrimination. Additionally, I include follow-up research from 2016 to illustrate how the 2015 global refugee crisis and the rise of far-right political parties, such as the Alternative for Germany (AfD), have reignited anti-foreigner racism in Germany, resulting in significant experiences of wariness, threat, racial stigma, and feelings of "perpetual foreignness" among Iranians in Germany.

Chapter 4 considers the ebbs and flows of racial projects, and how US and German nationalism comes and goes in severity. There are periods of time when explicit discourses and policies that promote prejudice and racism have been documented in both countries, most recently during the Trump administration. There have also been occasions when Americans believed they were "past race" or "post-racial," as seen during the Obama administration. Both covert and overt forms of racism and prejudice have a significant impact on how immigrants have chosen to identify themselves and live their lives, and these things have shaped their perceptions and experiences as they relate to race, belonging, and social membership. Thus, this chapter more deeply fleshes out the cumulative impact of existing racial projects and hierarchies on social citizenship and membership. It details how perceptions and experiences of belonging are relational and significantly shift according to sociopolitical climate and context. Lastly, I demonstrate how traumatic experiences of racial exclusion and racism have shaped how Iranians have coped with and responded to marginality, racialization, and politicization in both the US and Germany.

The book concludes with an examination of what the experiences of Iranians in the US and Germany can tell us about larger processes of racialization, racial boundaries, belonging and membership as they relate to global, regional, and national arrangements, movements, and policies. It also considers what may be in store for the future of US-Iran relations under the Biden administration, especially the fate of the Iran Deal.

1

Layered and Complicated

Migration and Settlement in the United States and Germany

Prior to the 1979 Iranian Revolution, the experiences of Iranian immigrants in the US and Germany did not differ significantly. The majority of those who had migrated were young men from families with financial resources in search of business, educational, and professional opportunities. Some experienced institutionalized settlement through a college or work, while others had no or very little institutional help. An Iranian passport was highly valued and visiting the US and Europe without a visa was commonplace. Iran's economic and political relations with Western nations, and the shah's modernization initiatives, meant that Iranians with financial means often traveled to the US and Europe to gain credentials and skills that would allow them to become more comfortable financially in Iran.

As I will show, the Iranian Revolution and the hostage crisis were pivotal in changing the experiences of Iranians in diaspora. Many of those living abroad did not foresee having to decide to stay permanently. Those who had left Iran during the social and political changes of the late 1970s and early 1980s "locked up their homes, packed a few suitcases, and viewed leaving as a temporary sojourn from their lives back in Iran, which would resume when the revolutionary government was overturned."[1] At this point, Iranians living in the US began to encounter direct and explicit anti-Iranian prejudice, racism, and hostility, while in Germany Iranians were received as political refugees.

I begin with a comparative analysis of Iran's relationship to Germany and the US in the past one hundred years, paying special attention to the economic and political relations between the nations prior to and after the Iranian Revolution and hostage crisis. I consider how the migration and settlement patterns of Iranians are impacted by the existence, or lack thereof, of universal asylum policy, especially since the revolution. Lastly, I underscore the fickleness and precariousness of belonging—where views and perceptions of an entire nation, culture, and people change virtually overnight. This begins a conversation, one that will continue throughout the subsequent chapters of this book, about how the racialization and politicization of Iranians, and their resulting social marginality, is deeply tied and susceptible to the social and political climate, domestically and globally.

Political and Economic Ties

Iran and Germany

The most prosperous period of Iranian-German relations was between the two world wars. Reza Pahlavi's British-backed military coup[2] against the Qajars from 1921 to 1926 resulted in his becoming the shah of Iran in 1926 and forming the Pahlavi dynasty. The partnership between Germany and Iran was reciprocal and beneficial for both nations. Germany was in search of global export markets and had a reputation for not getting involved in the domestic politics of other nations,[3] and Iran wanted to decrease the power of the two major superpowers, Russia and Britain, in controlling Iran's economic and political infrastructure (Khatib-Shahidi 2013). Foreign investors, loans, trade, and technological support were central to the launching of several industrialization and modernization projects.

Infrastructure Investment and Main Institutions

The creation of central institutions, including the national bank, the construction of railroads, and economic ventures were underway during the late 1920s and 1930s. Germany's interests in Iran were facilitated and extended through the creation in 1927 of the National Bank of Persia—now named Bank Melli and still operating as one of Iran's main banking institutions. The bank was a means to expand and further Germany's economic investments and political participation amid the longer role that the British and Russians played in Iran.[4] Germany was also a major contributor to the construction of the Trans-Iranian Railway that began in 1927 and was completed in 1938[5]. In 1935, trade agreements between Iran and Germany ensued and several extensive contracts were signed with German companies including Junkers, Siemens,[6] Holzmann, Krupp, I.G., Farben, and AED. The British-Russian invasion of Iran in 1941 caused Germany to lose almost all its political influence in Iran, although trade continued. After the withdrawal of Soviet troops from Iran in 1945, Germany would join the British and the US to guarantee its own security in the region.

In 1941, Reza Shah's son Mohammad Reza Shah took office and continued the economic and political relationship between the two nations.[7] Major German companies, like Siemens and Bosch, also continued to secure multimillion–deutsche mark contracts to help speed up Iranian industrialization and military modernization. In 1960 alone, Iran purchased more than half a billion deutsche marks worth of industrial equipment. Trade deals provided the Iranian government a strong lobby in cities like Bonn and Frankfurt.[8]

The West German government also bankrolled joint educational and scientific programs to raise the profile of Germany and strengthen the relationship between the nations. For example, the famous Goethe Institute[9] opened two branches in Iran—the first in Tehran in 1958 and the second in Shiraz in 1975. While the intention of this German-language training initially was to meet the demand for German instruction in Iran, it also became a place for Iranian artists, writers, musicians, and intellectuals to exhibit their work, arrange lectures, and show films. The institute also had relations with faculty at Iranian universities like the University of Tehran.[10]

Modernization policies also enabled the growth of a secular middle-class population that increasingly sent their children to Western institutions to study.[11] From 1959 onward, middle- and upper-class Iranians heavily emphasized the attainment of higher education, but the growing number of students could not be absorbed by the Iranian higher education system. Sending children abroad for higher education became increasingly commonplace throughout the 1960s and 1970s. Notably, these families were often secular and had positive views of the West.[12]

Iranian students would become the largest non-European group in West German education, and by the mid-1960s the majority of the 20,000 Iranians in Germany were either attending a university or had decided to settle in Germany after finishing their studies. This is reflected in the German census data. The first estimate of Iranians appears in 1963, when reportedly 750 Iranians had been admitted that year. Between 1961 and 1970, a total of 7,298 Iranian nationals entered Germany. The number of Iranians who migrated to Germany doubled between 1971 and 1980, reaching 14,173.[13] While we have no census data on the economic background of these Iranians, the majority were middle-class and able to afford living and studying abroad. These migrants were also different than the image and stereotype of the "guest worker" that saturated Germany; only a small number of Iranians came to Germany as migrant workers.

Iran and the US

European powers, especially the British, Germans, French, and Russians, each had their share of economic power and influence in Iran. It was the overthrow of the democratically elected prime minister, Mohammad Mossadegh, in August 1953 by the CIA, with the backing of the then shah of Iran, Mohammad Reza Pahlavi, that greatly changed the relationship between Iran and the US. The coup was a response to the Iranian parliament and Mossadegh's decision to expel foreign corporate representatives and nationalize Iran's oil industry in 1951. The nationalization of Iranian oil created much outcry around the world, and the British created a global campaign to garner support for the boycotting of Iranian oil, even taking it to the UN and the International Court of

Justice.[14] The prime minister of Iran passionately defended national sovereignty and Iran's right to have control over its natural resources; the British and the Americans were not pleased. "Operation Ajax" marked the first time the US had covertly toppled a foreign government during peacetime. Dabashi (2007) argues that the overthrow is "the most traumatic event in modern Iranian history, a trauma from which the people have yet to recover" (p. 127). The overthrow of Mossadegh had a significant impact on Iranian political and civic life as it gave the shah power to rule more firmly as a monarch. From the coup onward, the US would play a central role in shaping Iranian economic and political policy.[15]

Oil and Education

Western oil companies returned under the International Oil Consortium Agreement of 1954, by which British Petroleum[16] and several American and French companies attained 40 percent ownership of Iran's oil production.[17] The shah's vision for Iran's future included significant foreign-backed economic modernization and cultural westernization. From 1953 until 1979, Pahlavi family members, business elites, the military all benefited from the shah's economic initiatives. The West, in particular the US, benefitted from its economic relationship in tangible and intangible ways. This included foreign employment and investment opportunities, secure oil supplies, and having a lobby through the shah in OPEC.[18] Similar to German banks, America's banking system also played a critical role in increasing America's economic role in Iran.[19] Iran was also a significant purchaser of US military weapons, airplanes, and consumer products. In 1977 alone, US exports to Iran were estimated at over one billion dollars.[20]

One of the main pillars of the shah's modernization program was an investment in international education, especially in engineering, science, and technology. Western-trained Iranians were vital for the promotion of national development and innovation, and one of the major ways this was achieved was through supporting and funding of international study and training.[21] In describing the important role of American educational institutions in the modernization program in Iran, Shannon (2015) underscores the role of the Ford Foundation in providing US-educated Iranian economists and intellectuals opportunities to study abroad. There were many in Iran, including many prominent scholars, who believed that education was the main pathway to Iran's modernization.

The first wave of Iranian immigration to the US is attributed to the growing relations between the nations. Prior to 1960, the total number of Iranians in the US stood at 3,459. Between 1960 and 1969, a total of 10,720 Iranians migrated to the US, placing the total estimate of Iranians at 13,450. By 1979, that figure grew to 49,192.[22] A Migration Policy Institute report estimated that "in the 1977–1978 academic year, about 100,000 Iranians were studying abroad . . . of whom 36,220 were enrolled in US institutes of higher learning; the rest were mainly in the United Kingdom, West Germany, France, Austria, and Italy." By the following academic year, that figure increased to 45,340 and peaked at 51,310 in 1979–1980.[23]

Pre-revolution Settlement

In detailing the settlement experiences of those who came prior to the revolution, I consider the critical role of political diplomacy in facilitating institutional ties and relationships that allowed Iranians to visit Germany and the US without a visa, and the ease with which Iranians were able to attain academic and professional opportunities in both Germany and the US. An Iranian passport was considered a national treasure, and with it many traveled through Western nations without a visa.[24]

Choices and Opportunities

Foreign policy, institutional ties, support, and a more positive reception stand out in the experiences of pre-revolution migrants. Political and economic alliances and relations made the attainment of a visa to study or business fairly easy, and those with financial means or institutional support migrated to the US or Europe[25] in growing numbers. Modernization initiatives encouraged and funded the education of Iranians in Western educational institutions.[26] In some cases, the college or university organized their settlement, and in other cases, students made their own arrangements with the financial support of their families. There were also agencies that assisted Iranians with the college application process for studying abroad. Some intended on returning to Iran after the completion of their degrees,[27] while others wanted to stay permanently. Another set of Iranians came to and from Iran on a regular basis[28] for business.

Iranians were overwhelmingly perceived as "friendly foreigners" and felt that the doors of opportunity were open to them. The ease in travel and migration and the advancement of educational and professional endeavors is reflected in the stories of my interlocutors. When asked why they left Iran, first-generation respondents commonly described education as a main motivation. Cyrus, a first-generation professional living in southern California, explained:

> I went to Sharif University in 1969, and maybe three or four months later, I suddenly decided to come to the US, and at the time all of my family was in Iran. . . . I had a friend and he was the same—we went to high school together and also same the same university in Iran, and his brother was telling us how America was and everything was fair, and it was great here, his brother lived here. Everyone here is so free and at that time there were a lot of issues with the Iranian government. These were strange times in Iran; with the situation of the gasoline prices going up and there were demonstrations, and they were burning the buses. It was a tense moment at the time.

Those in Iran often heard stories from friends and family—some true and some exaggerated—about what life in the US was like and the opportunities that were available. Compared to Iran's more uncertain sociopolitical climate, the US was considered a free and democratic nation, a place for opportunity and fairness. Cyrus had graduated top of his class from Sharif University—considered to be Iran's top university for engineering and the physical sciences—which had gotten him into a PhD program at the University of Southern California. His settlement was fully institutionalized, and he did not worry about having to secure housing or other necessities upon arrival. While his international student status had exempted him from receiving educational scholarships, his parents provided financial support. At the time, he felt that these earlier experiences reinforced what he had heard about the US; America was a land of opportunity and a place where immigrants could succeed.

State support and encouragement of Western education also shows up in the prevalence of agencies dedicated to helping Iranians apply to American colleges. Michael, a first-generation Iranian man living in northern California, described how these college-placement agencies helped him migrate to the US in the 1970s:[29]

> Before I left Iran, I had all these acceptance letters, and one was Glenside. There were these companies and agencies that specialized in locating colleges in the US and get[ting] you your papers and admission. So I had my papers for Glenside, but I had to leave quickly because I was supposed to serve in the military. Went I got to Glenside I took some language courses. I had another acceptance letter for Detroit for a summer session. I had no clue what Detroit was about. So I went to Detroit, and it was not what I expected; I did not like it. So I had a third admission letter for Stanislaus, because they had me choose a school in California. So I got on the bus and headed for California.

Michael arrived in 1977 with acceptance letters from three American colleges. His application, student visa, and admission to college were all processed through this agency. Without it, coming to the US for school would have been more challenging. Michael had the opportunity to visit each institution before choosing the one in California. He told me that the good things he had heard about California is what convinced him that he should settle there. When I asked him about his settlement experiences, he explained:

> I did it all on my own. I didn't know anybody. What I did was when I was in Detroit, I contacted the dorm manager and made sure that he had a room for me. I had no family and friends there. And then when I got to Turlock, I took the bus. I could have flown but I wanted to see the country. I had time. The bus ride from Detroit to Turlock was a long one. And once I got there, I called the dorm manager, and he came to pick me up.

Like others at the time, Michael had also come to the US to further his education. He had access to housing in the form of student dorms but did not have financial support from his family or family and friend networks. He also obtained an on-campus job shortly after arriving to financially support himself. Compared to Iranians like Cyrus who were financially supported by their families in Iran, he faced more financial challenges. Throughout my conversation with Michael, I also had the impression that having experienced a lack of support and community in the US meant that he only had himself to rely upon, and that this had reinforced the notion that America was truly a place where one is afforded the opportunity to become "self-made" and "pull yourself up by the bootstraps." He felt that if he could make it in America anyone can.

Like those who went to the US, those in Germany were also in pursuit of greater educational opportunities. Ali, a first-generation professional, told me the following about why he migrated in 1978:

> When I lived in Iran, I met this research group from the University of Hamburg that did the type of work that I was doing in Iran. Research work relating to taking measurements of the earth, determining the layers of the earth, what type of materials are underneath the earth, like geophysics. When they saw my work, they liked it, and insisted that I go to Germany. I was not in agreement, because I had gotten a scholarship

to go to UC Berkeley for my PhD. Once they found this out, the research group got in contact with the German research organization to invite me over. They invited us to go to Germany and agreed to pay all the tuition and money that the Iranian government was going to pay the US, and all the expenses like learning German, and for my wife. I went to Hamburg and from the beginning, you may not believe this, but from the beginning they placed me in this very office from the first day.

German scientists and engineers were in Iran doing research during the time that Ali was an undergraduate student. This research group was so impressed by him that they offered him an acceptance letter and financial support, despite his having accepted an offer from UC Berkeley. He ultimately chose the program at the University of Hamburg as the financial package was a better one—it also aided his wife, in the form of German-language courses, which convinced him to choose Germany over the US. Importantly, Ali and his family were also provided housing, not in the form of graduate student housing, but rather a nice apartment in Blankenese, a mostly German part of Hamburg. He was also given a generous-sized office that he still inhabited until his retirement in 2016.[30] He told me that this initial welcome had made him feel wanted, respected, and as someone they saw as a professional, otherwise they would not have "invested in him the way that they had." His more than thirty-year academic career was very research active, and the vast resources available to him[31] were further evidence that he was an important and valued member of the University of Hamburg and larger German society.

Another set of Iranians came to Germany for work; business ties between Iran and the West meant that employment abroad was feasible and uncomplicated. Western companies played a key role in facilitating this, and Iranians, especially middle-class ones, were able to leave Iran and seek employment opportunities. Houshang explained how his ability to work[32] in the US in the early 1970s—and eventually migrate to Germany to study—was connected to his work history with Americans in Iran:

I worked at an aluminum company. One of their partners was Reynolds aluminum, from the USA, and all the aluminum belonged to them. This company sent me to the USA, to Arkansas, to a city called Malvern. I was there for six months and worked in a chemical laboratory. Then I returned to Iran and worked at company in the city of Arak. I was there for two years. All the bosses there were Americans. I then decided that I wanted to go to the USA to continue my education, but then I came to Hamburg and saw that they were also building a company here. The boss of the company in Arak was American and wrote a letter to the Hamburg office and told them to hire me. I was supposed to go to the USA, however a friend of mine who was working in the USA but had trained in Hamburg told me that Germany was better. . . . He also said that Germany is closer to Iran in case I wanted to return. So I went to Hamburg, got hired there, and the next day after my arrival I went to work.

The centrality of business ties is reflected in Houshang's experiences of working in Iran, the US, and Germany. Iranians, like Houshang, were able to work in the US and Europe through foreign-trade policies and expansive business deals that were made possible through political relationships between Iran and Western nations. His work experiences with Americans living and working in Iran provide a clear example of the extent of economic and political relations between the nations. Houshang's point that all his supervisors in Iran were American is supported by estimates of foreign employment in Iran prior to the revolution. Fatemi (1980) estimates that in the summer of 1978, one-third of workers in Iranian oil and oil-related industries were American.

Having a choice between going to the US or Europe was common for Iranians prior to the revolution. Pari also recounted an educational journey that took her from Iran to the UK and eventually to Germany in 1974 to study architecture. She recounted:

In 1974, many Iranian students were arriving. My parents still did not want me to stay, because they thought I was an unsupervised young woman in Germany. In England, they thought I was working in a company and under some supervision. They thought I would be less protected here. So I returned to Iran, and I told them that I wanted to study there, work there.

In the 1960s and 1970s there were increasing numbers of Iranians coming to Germany to study; Pari was one of them. She was one of the few women in my research that had migrated alone—without a spouse, friends, or family—prior to the revolution. It was not yet the norm for single women to migrate without existing family and networks. She went on to detail the arduous process of convincing her parents to give her permission to study in Germany:

> I would work on them every day. In Iran, I worked two jobs, took language classes at the Goethe Institute in Tehran so that I could work on my language skills. I was able to continue my German quite well. It was expensive, but the schooling was very good; it was a stellar education. I stayed in Iran from January until August of 1974, took courses for four months. The certificate I got from Iran was better than those I would have received here, and it allowed me to go to the university. I convinced my parents that I would go to Germany, and that I would be safe. And to make them feel better, I decided to go to a small city, not Berlin. So that's how I then ended up in Goettingen.

Women seldom traveled or migrated abroad without their families. Unlike her male counterparts, Pari had to prove her commitment and dedication to her family because getting their blessing was no small feat. It was not until she got a German language-certificate from the well-respected Goethe Institute, was working the equivalent of a full-time job, and assured them that she would move to a small college town that she received their approval. It is notable that none of the men who had come during the same time in either country spoke of having to convince their parents and family to go abroad; rather, they were encouraged to do so.

The rise of domestic uprisings and anti-shah protests in the late 1970s motivated migration and changed its routes and patterns. Attaining a US visas was increasingly difficult by the late 1970s, which meant that Iranians began to migrate to Canada and European countries in greater numbers. These political uncertainties also meant that critical decisions were often made on a whim. Kimia, a first-generation woman who had lived in Germany for more than three decades, said this about her migration:

> I left the beginning of 1978, and the revolution in Iran had just started to take shape and be underway. I had just gotten my high school diploma and about four months before the revolution I came to Germany with the intent of going to the US. . . . The whole time, my intent was to go to the US because my sister was there. She had gone there from Iran and been able to get the visa. My situation hit the revolution and I was not able to go. We were supposed to be in the US together. I tried to get a visa from Germany to the US, and they told me that I had to get it through Iran. I learned German here for a while. I was a young woman and I had come by myself, and the only person that was here was my uncle. When I saw that the US wasn't going to happen, I stayed here.

Kimia's story is like those of many Iranians I have encountered in Germany who had family who had gone to the US before the revolution. While her plan was to join her sister and maternal family members in the US, and pursue her education there, this coincided with the onset of the revolution, which made entry to the US nearly impossible. After multiple unsuccessful attempts she decided to remain in Germany and attended the University of Hamburg instead.[33]

As illustrated, trade agreements, foreign investments, and support for the creation of central institutions, like banks, is always political. Economic interests help further particular political objectives. Prior to the revolution the migration experiences of Iranians were mostly uncomplicated because of existing political and economic relations between the nations. A set of policies and programs were in place to encourage and support cross-national business and education ventures, tourism, and travel, and those who were male and middle-class, especially, found the US and Germany to be a place of opportunity and upward mobility. The gender restrictions within Iranian families made it difficult for un-married single women to move and live abroad without family supervision.[34] After the Iranian Revolution the experiences of Iranians began to diverge in significant ways. The social and political portrayal of and feeling toward Iranians differed by national context. In Germany, Iranians were overwhelmingly received as political asylum seekers and refugees whereas in the US Iranians they were depicted as "hostage takers" and "enemy foreigners."

Post-revolution Settlement

The 1979 Iranian Revolution removed Mohammad Reza Pahlavi from office, and on November 4, 1979, the US Embassy in Tehran was taken over and approximately fifty American staff members were held hostage for 444 days. Diplomatic ties between the US and Iran were severed, which resulted in extensive economic sanctions, the freezing of Iranian assets, and the stoppage of visas to Iranian nationals. The severing of political ties also meant that the educational and professional initiatives that Iranians took advantage of—and the primary method by which they had migrated to the US in the pre-revolution period—were now gone.

Many left Iran because of the uncertain social and political climate. Some were in direct conflict with the newly formed government and had to leave; this included royalists and supporters of the shah, religious minorities, intellectuals, political activists, and artists. Others employed by state institutions found it difficult to work with the new government and were compelled to leave. Some Iranians left with extensive economic resources, while others, especially working-class students, faced great challenges in their settlement.

Surveillance at Home and Abroad

After the revolution, the US government regarded Iran as a "core country of Islamic fundamentalism."[35] This climate was especially traumatic for Iranians living in the US. They were accused of supporting Khomeini, "the Mullahs," and Islamists. This is reflected in the direct and explicit anti-Iranian racism and prejudice that permeated American popular culture. From a 1989 *Saturday Night Live* comedy skit titled "The Iranian Family Court," in which white actors "portray Iranians" in a racist and humanizing manner, to "Khomeini toilet paper" and music recordings such as Bobby B. Baker's "Take Your Oil and Shove It" and Roger Hallmark and the Thrasher Brothers' "A Message to Khomeini," anti-Iranian sentiment was front and center in American popular culture.[36] During and after the revolution and hostage crisis, there was also a steady rise of TV news specials and feature films that Naficy (2012) calls "Crisis Journalism" and "Captivity Narratives." This included the fictional movie *Not Without My Daughter*[37] and TV shows titled *Iran: The Desperate Dilemma, American Held Hostage, A Year in Captivity, Families Held Hostage,* and a number of others that aired on major TV networks such as ABC, CBS, and NBC.[38] The nightly news also heavily focused on the "Iran story," as seen by the number of minutes dedicated to "covering Iran."[39] Iranians living in the US were persistently associated with this discourse and became targets of state surveillance.[40] Iranian college students were deported or at risk of deportation. This made settlement more precarious, strenuous, and complicated, and it also made Iranians more susceptible to experiences of exclusion and discrimination. Iranians had seemingly gone from being "friendly foreigners to foreign enemies"[41] almost overnight, and these transformations are vividly present in their lived experiences.

Many of my interlocutors experienced drastic shifts in this social climate. They experienced themselves becoming "enemy foreigners" and "hostage takers." They described a sense of being increasingly watched and harassed in public—there was a lot of resentment toward Iran and

Iranians, and it was palpable. The settlement experiences of Iranians living in the US in this time were extremely uncertain, many not knowing whether they would be allowed to stay in the US or deported back to Iran. They were also deeply concerned about further tensions between Iran and the US. Mary, a first-generation woman living in northern California, described her experiences as an international college student in Florida:

> They had no idea about Iran beside the hostages and what was in the media. So there was a lot of resentment with me at the dorms. It was in my second year where I used to get snide remarks, like when my roommate told me that she did not want to live with that Iranian and that she was going to ask for a transfer and all that. A couple of instances where there was some spray painting of the door. I was frightened and, um, and amazingly I had already made some connections with a couple of girls in my street. They were Americans—they offered a lot of support and one of them offered her parents' house. I wanted to live off campus, and that opportunity was amazing.

Mary's explicit mention of the media is significant. It reflects how powerful the "Iran story" was throughout the US, and how the image of Iranians as "hostage takers" had profound consequences for Iranians, as they began to become targets of state surveillance,[42] deportation, and interpersonal racism. It was not rare for private citizens, ordinary Americans, to explicitly let Iranians knows that they were "watching them" or that they were not welcome in America anymore. Mary experienced direct forms of racism, and she talked about how the hostage crisis had created a scary and tense environment for Iranians:

> At the time there was a lot of deportations of Iranians and all these Iranian guys from engineering and computer department, and they were being shipped back to Iran. I was so afraid. My student advisor had told me that someone had contacted them with a list of Iranians. I was a good

student; I was maintaining As and Bs despite the forty-hour workload. He suggested that I be very careful and that the officers are coming back in ten days, so that gave me an unsettling state. One of the girls offered her boyfriend to marry me [she laughs], so that's what I did; I didn't want to risk going back.

The "Iranian Control Program," which led to the deportation of Iranian students, involved the screening of approximately fifty-seven thousand Iranian students. It was mandatory and required registering with the Immigration and Naturalization Service (INS)—whose functions are now under the Department of Homeland Security (DHS)—and providing a valid student visa and proof of full-time student status.[43] Mary had a valid student visa and a high grade point average, but the breakdown of diplomatic relations between the Iranian government and the US posed serious problems for her and other Iranian international students. She witnessed Iranians being deported and was warned by college administrators and faculty to make sure to keep a low profile. Also, while she does not address this directly, gender certainly played a factor too, especially given the gendered stereotypes of Muslim and Middle Eastern men as being radical, uncivilized, violent, and anti-Western. Mary was unsettled by the conversation with her college counselor and the fear around being deported led her to make some drastic decisions—she married her friend's boyfriend to become a US citizen. Mary's experiences were not uncommon. Several other first-generation interviewees who were in the US in the late 1970s and early 1980s also attained US citizenship by marrying an American to avoid potential deportation. Nick, a first-generation Iranian who was an international student at the University of Washington, shared vivid memories of the hostage crisis:

I suffered when the hostages were taken. I was a college student, in my second year of college in 1979. There were nineteen to twenty Iranian students in the college. We got word from our advisor, and he took us to his office and said, "You all better be careful, you're lucky you live in Seattle, not like California or NY, but there are still people out there that don't like foreigners, there are rednecks everywhere, racists everywhere, be careful if you go somewhere, and go together."

The portrayal of Iranians as "hostage takers" had dire consequences for the Iranian community. Anti-Iranian racism was palpable, and Iranians were aggressively and violently profiled because their homeland was associated with the taking of American hostages. Again, we see the mention of Iranian college students being explicitly warned by college professors and school officials that Americans were angry with Iranians over the hostage crisis, and that going to public places could be dangerous. Even though Nick lived in a seemingly liberal city, racism was everywhere and all those who looked like they are "from there" were potential targets of racial violence. Every night, across the country, Americans were watching the same images of Iranians taking over the embassy and burning the American flag while chanting "Death to America."

Iranians were transformed into foreign enemies almost overnight; indeed, the portrayal and racialization of Iranians as "savages," as "hostage takers," and an "enemy race" is a part of a long line of racial projects targeting those from Muslim-majority nations and South West Asia and North Africa (SWANA), also known as the "Middle East."[44] The experiences of Iranians during this time period this is a powerful example of how racialization and politicization changes and intensifies according to social political climate. It also speaks to how preexisting racisms and prejudices become activated by domestic and global policies and events. The mandatory registration calls by the INS noted in the experiences of Iranians during the hostage crisis would be echoed by DHS after September 11, 2001.[45]

I offer another example of how institutional ties have impacted the lives of Iranians by sharing the story of Mansoor, a first-generation Iranian immigrant residing in southern California. His migration story and how he ultimately gained permanent residency for himself and his family in the US point to my ongoing conversation about the role of global political ties and foreign policy in the migration and settlement experiences of Iranians. All state-run institutions had been affected by the changes in the Iranian government, and Mansoor worked in the aviation industry. He told me that those early years after the revolution were tense and that the workplace had changed—all the workers were being watched, and there was a climate of suspicion about who was loyal to the new government. He recounted several instances where he had gotten in trouble at work and how he felt "under surveillance" and even worried about his safety. Like many who could not legally leave Iran, Mansoor obtained a passport and visas through a middleman and went to Germany. Once there, with the help of the international rescue committee,[46] he applied for and was eventually granted political asylum in the US. When I asked what was required to qualify for this organization's help, he explained:

> For the US, in the 1980s there were four requirements, because we were not refugees, and we were not immigrants. They had four requirements: one, was to be a religious minority; two, having first-class family member here; three, having work experience with Americans; and I don't remember the fourth one. In Iran, I did work with Americans, but I did not work for them, I worked with them. So when international rescue committee asked me this, I said I had documents issued by helicopter companies that were counterparts of Iranian companies that worked with Iranians.

We see the role of business ties with American companies and his previous work relationship with American aviation companies come into play in Mansoor's asylum case. Past work experience made his case eligible for official refugee status. Importantly, he told me that the International Rescue Committee provided him institutionalized help, which involved housing in southern California, permission to work, and a path toward permanent residency. Mansoor had a short stay in Germany before he was granted asylum in the US, and this gave me the opportunity to ask why he migrated to the US as opposed to staying in Germany. He explained:

> Germany is heaven for Germans, not for foreigners. I had friends there; you know as a foreigner, it was extremely difficult to get into my career, because they have priority there. If you came from a commonwealth country, like a European one, you would have priority.

His decision to permanently settle in the US was influenced by his experiences in Germany, the experiences of friends, and residing in refugee housing for three years. Like others who had been to Germany, Mansoor felt it to be "heaven for Germans," but a society that was cold and unwelcoming toward non-Germans and non-Europeans. He also expected that finding employment in his profession would be difficult, given the industry's preference for German or European workers. He also felt that, in Germany, race/ethnicity and national origins mattered more in shaping opportunities for mobility than in the US, which is why he ultimately chose to move himself and his family to California, even though their asylum case had been approved by the time they migrated to the US.

After the hostage crisis, Iranians had limited options for legally entering the US. The majority of Iranians who have come in the post-revolution era have done so through family reunification and H1N1 visas, as well as the green card lottery.[47] Iranians who were unable to obtain a US visa often went to other European nations, like Germany, or applied for asylum in the US via another country.[48] Unlike past waves that consisted mostly of individual students and professionals, the post-revolution wave included entire families, many of whom were political refugees and exiles.

As illustrated, the lives of Iranians in the US changed drastically in the pre- and post-revolution years. The difficulties of attaining a US visa and the absence of a universal asylum policy have made the migration of Iranians into the US more complicated and difficult than prior to the revolution. Moreover, Iranians were being increasingly racialized and associated with an Islamist government, and their settlement was greatly informed by a social and political climate that was increasingly marginalizing them. Undoubtedly, the hostage crisis years also left scars and have had considerable implications for how Iranians have identified with their Iranian ancestry, with being Muslim, with being "from the Middle East," with race and racial categorization, with community building, and their pathways toward integration. As I will show in chapter 4, these earlier experiences have shaped inclinations and efforts of wanting to be racially ambiguous and go under "the racial radar" as a means of escaping marginality, discrimination, and racism.

Asylum Seekers

The impact of the Iranian Revolution was felt differently in Germany. While the German government did not necessarily prefer the newly established government, this did not mean that the Iranian embassy in Germany would be closed, that flights between the nations would cease, that visas to German would be halted, or that Iranian students would be deported. The difficulties of attaining a US visa meant that Iranians increasingly migrated to refugee-accepting nations, like Canada, Germany, or the Netherlands. The motives for migration and the methods by which Iranians left were varied; some had been politically active and feared for their lives while others had lost friends and family members and feared for their safety and future. Those who could leave on a visa did, while others were smuggled out of the country. Post-revolution Iranian migrants' economic backgrounds were also more diverse and there were more working-class individuals and families. From the early 1980s onward, steady flows of Iranians migrated to Germany.[49] According to the German census between 1981 and 1990, 67,022 Iranians were admitted to Germany—almost five times the figure in the previous decade.[50] According to a report published by UNHCR, between the years of 1995 and 2011, 44,806 Iranians sought asylum in Germany.[51] In the years 2014–2019, UNHCR data shows a steady flow of asylum seekers: a total of 18,484 applications were received and 4,287 Iranians granted asylum.[52] The Organization for Economic Co-operation and Development (OECD) estimated that between 2000 and 2013, a total of 75,237 Iranian nationals applied for asylum,[53] and in a more recent report titled "Finding their Way," the OECD indicates that there was a total of 31,820 asylum applications from Iran nationals between 2015 and 2016. The difference between 2015 and 2016 is striking; there were 5,394 applications in 2015, while the following year there was an exponential increase to 26,426.[54]

Germany continues to be a prime destination for Iranian asylum seekers mostly because of its universal asylum policy and refugee resettlement program. Once asylum seekers reach the border, they can apply for asylum and have their case heard before the asylum court. They are provided with housing, medical care, and sometimes language courses while they await their interview. When I asked Iranians to describe how Germany receives immigrants there was almost an immediate mention of it being a nation that receives refugees, but not one that accepts immigrants. For example, Houshang explained that:

> immigration does not exist here unless there's a company that wants to hire you. The company would either require you to have a German passport or the foreigner would have to receive a work permit here. This person would have to be hired for this to happen. That's one instance for migration. The second one would be through seeking asylum. And in article 20, if in your own nation you are subject to racial, religious, or political discrimination persecution you can seek asylum here.

There are two ways to migrate to Germany, either being hired by a German company—like Houshang had done—or through seeking asylum. By law, the state must accept refugee seekers; it does not accept them "voluntarily" per se. While he does not explicitly say this, the constitutional mandate (article 20) to accept asylum seekers is directly connected to Nazism in Germany. Iranians frequently mention that "Germany is forced by law" to accept refugees and that German society does not necessarily "willingly" or "happily" accept them. For Houshang, this clarification is an important one because it shapes the nature by which one is seen and accepted; are you a professional that is recruited for your skills or are you being provided refuge because you are escaping persecution?

Those who had been politically active in Iran and fled to Germany for asylum overwhelmingly described it as a humanitarian nation and viewed their larger settlement through this perspective. Heide, a first-generation woman living in Hamburg since the mid-1980s, had been active in a leftist political organization and had served time in prison in Iran because of it. Her children had been taken from her, she was placed in a mental asylum in Iran, and she had to sign papers stating that she would cease her activism to be released. She ultimately hired someone to smuggle her out of Iran in 1983 and applied for asylum upon arriving in Germany. Her children would join her several years later. She explained why she considered Germany to be a social welfare state:

> The system that Germany has, which I have experienced after being here for these years, is that Germany is truly a social state, a social welfare state. . . . They will get you a place to live, food, an income. Until your case gets approved, this is the process.

Germany is a place that grants refuge to those escaping persecution, and refugee resettlement is fully institutionalized by the state—housing, healthcare, and food are all provided for. The way Heide was received and treated in Germany, and the opportunities she had been afforded the last thirty-plus years, had affirmed that Germany was a humanitarian society. As a matter of fact, she believed in and trusted German institutions so much that she had been working as a social worker for the asylum and refugee office in the city of Hamburg the past two decades.

She told me that she saw first-hand what Germany did for refugees and this had proven to her that Germany was committed to humanitarian principles and policies.

Iranians who were not politically active also found themselves implicated in situations that compelled them to leave Iran. Shahin, a first-generation Iranian man who had lived in Hamburg for over two decades, described the circumstances that facilitated his family's migration in 1988:

> I did not have political problems in Iran, but my brother did. And because my brother was executed, I was forced to leave; there was not much I could do. I was doing well in Iran, but I had to leave it all, sell it all off.

After the revolution, state repression was widespread and many who were opposed to the newly established government found themselves imprisoned or executed. While Shahin was not political, his brother was, and his death made it impossible for him to stay in Iran. He was not concerned for himself but had a wife and a young child and could not risk their safety. He had been doing well in Iran, and migrating had considerably impacted his family's financial well-being. In our interview, he spoke at length about having to make decisions between financial comfort as opposed to social and political freedom, and he believed that his wife and children had benefitted the most from their migration. This was something I heard on numerous occasions from other first-generation Iranian men: that they had lost businesses, property, and the value of their educational degrees in the process of starting all over again. They felt that their migration had led to their downward mobility, financially and professionally, but had benefitted their wives and especially their children.

Iran's post-revolution social and political climate was repeatedly mentioned as a main motivation for leaving, especially the limited social and political freedoms for young people. Buye Gandom, a first-generation woman studying engineering at the University of Hamburg, described

the larger circumstances that caused her to leave Iran in 2000. This ultimately led to the migration of her mother, her sixteen-year-old brother,
and herself. She spoke to me about the anxiety-filled, arduous journey
to Germany, which involved a smuggler who took them to the Ukraine.
They tried to get a family visa into Greece, but she was not approved, so
her brother and mother went instead. She stayed in the Ukraine for a
little bit, applied for a visa to Brazil, and through paid connections traveled through Austria. It was in Vienna that she boarded a train to Hamburg and applied for asylum upon arriving in Germany. She recounted
her asylum case and the details of her hearing:

> He asked me a lot of questions; about my political participation in the
> organization, all the things I did. They gave me a break so that I could
> eat, and my nerves were wrecked. The translator came and then we spoke
> until about 6:00 p.m. It was all taped. And then they shut down the tape
> and the guy wanted to personally talk to me. Until about 8:00 p.m., he
> was just asking me why we were disappointed in Khatami, what had hap-
> pened, the political process there, why our expectations were not met. It
> was very interesting. His wife was Iranian, and he was a very good man
> and human being. And for about two hours he spoke to me. He also told
> me that he was not supposed to tell me yet, but that he had approved my
> case. I was so excited and happy when I left there.

Iranians, especially younger ones, had vested hope in the reformist president Mohammad Khatami. While his candidacy relaxed and expanded
some social freedoms, ultimately young people were disappointed in the
lack of substantive progressive changes. Buye Gandom's involvement in
student-led organizations on her university campus caused her many
troubles. It was this, along with continued surveillance and social and
political suppression, which led Buye Gandom, and numerous others,
to seek ways to leave Iran and migrate to nations that were known to
accept refugees and asylum seekers. A few things also stand out from
Buye Gandom's description of her asylum case hearing. Namely, her

depiction of the German asylum officer and his inquiries about the circumstances of Iranians. Obviously, he is connected to and familiar with Iran by being married to an Iranian. But Buye Gandom's portrayal of the hearing officer as educated, someone "who wants to know more," and a "good human being" is significant, because one often hears Iranians in Germany make remarks like, "Germans are more sophisticated and educated than Americans, and Germans know how to distinguish between different peoples and cultures." This sentiment is salient in both the interviews and the larger fieldwork and stands in great contrast to what I have heard from Iranians: that Americans—by whom they mean white Americans—act like "cowboys." Iranians in the US do not necessarily see Americans as empathizing with them or lamenting the things that have befallen them—no one cares about the larger circumstances of their migration to the US. In chapter 4, I unpack and analyze how these exchanges and interactions with Germans have facilitated a feeling among Iranians that they are a different kind of refugee.[55]

The migration and settlement experiences of the interviewed Iranians have been shaped by the circumstances of their departure from Iran, their mode of settlement, the available resources for settlement, and the type of climate they encountered. Those who left Iran prior to the revolution did so for educational and professional opportunities, while those who left after had mostly social and political motives. Their settlement experiences in both nations were mixed; some had prearranged institutionalized help in the form of tuition assistance and student housing, while others had no assistance. There were cases of institutionalized settlement in both the US and Germany. The interviews also showed that Iranians preferred the US; those in Germany and the US described it as a democratic society that provided real opportunity and equality to all. This perception was rooted in the idea that "race did not matter in the US," because it was a nation of immigrants, a melting pot.

Discussion

Foreign policy considerations make the difference between diplomacy or military conflict and war, inclusion or exclusion, and the intensity of racial and political stigmatization. Pre-revolution Iranian migrants were mostly students and professionals who had come to the US and German to further educational and professional goals. These opportunities were made possible because of favorable political relations between Iran and Western nations. Iranians were welcome in Western nations. The Iranian Revolution and the hostage crisis changed some of these dynamics, especially for Iranians in the US. After the revolution and hostage crisis stark dissimilarities arise in the settlement experiences of Iranians. In one context they were treated like an enemy and the other as a refugee; this is considerably tied to each nation's relationship with Iran—past and present.

In the US, the racialization and politicization of Iranians was in high gear, and the depiction of Iranians as "hostage takers" had dire implications. Said (1981) argues that the "Iran story" was how most Americans came to "know" Iran and Iranians, and that it was constructed through "an incredibly detailed, highly focused attention of the media to the event and Iran's demonization for years after it" (p. 81). Importantly, it was not just the racial othering and racialization of Iranians that was taking place but rather that the "Iran story" was regarded as news "about Islam." In the words of Said, "Iran came to symbolize represented American relations with the Muslim world" (p. 83) and that in many ways "the loss of Iran to an Islamic form of government was the greatest setback the United States had had in recent years" (p. 84).

The severing of diplomatic relations drastically changed American immigration policy toward Iran, as well as Iranians' sense of safety and security in the US. The US government did not consider Iranians to be political exiles or as people in need of refuge. Asylum policy toward Iranians was not universal in nature and did not often grant Iranians official refugee status. Historically, being politically allied with the US has generally meant generous provisions for resettlement,[56] as seen in the case of earlier waves of Cuban exiles that came during the Cuban Revolution and received generous federal assistance for settlement.[57] This was not the case for Iranians.

Moreover, with the closure of the US embassy in Iran, Iranians could no longer apply for an immigrant, student, or tourist visa, making migration increasingly difficult. Unless they immigrated with a school or work visa or through family ties, migration was hardly feasible. Iranians were also often profiled by the INS and subject to deportation during the revolution and hostage crisis years. Growing anti-Iranian sentiment in the US also led Iranians to be verbally and physically attacked, and for many these memories were lying dormant, and, as I discuss, reawakened with the presidency of Donald Trump. The Iranian Revolution, the hostage crisis, and the precarious political relationship between the US and Iran over the past four decades have had a lasting impact on Iranians' sense of place and belonging, as well as the kinds of communities that they have created, in the US.

In Germany, Iranians attained permanent residency mostly through seeking asylum, and their settlement experiences reflects this. The growth of a sizeable Iranian community in Germany was precisely due to Germany's universal asylum policy. Institutionalized support for refugee resettlement and access to the social insurance system is what led Iranians to experience the German state as a refugee-accepting nation that provided migrants with settlement assistance and legal protection. This reinforced the image of Germany as a socially democratic nation that is humanitarian in its policies. This narrative has increased since the asylum crisis of the 1990s as well as when Germany accepted over 1.2 million refugees in the aftermath of the 2015 refugee crisis. Still inconsistencies remain; Germany is a refugee-accepting society that maintains deep-rooted anti-foreigner and anti-Muslim racism and prejudice.

Moreover, being accepted as a refugee in Germany does not mean that the doors to economic mobility are as open as they are to the native German population. European scholars have stressed that national context plays an important part in shaping integration.[58] Crul and Schneider (2009), for example, underscore how different educational institutional arrangements across European nations greatly affect achievement and mobility among immigrants and their children.[59] As I show in chapter 3, Iranian immigrants and their children also face barriers to educational and economic mobility in Germany, especially in the academic track and vocational programs. This is less about their own skills, merit, or achievements and more about the institutional arrangements in the German national context.

As Iranians began to settle into their new communities, they gained more insight into the nations they had migrated to. How would the larger national and global context shape and influence their lives? In the next three chapters, I trace Iranians' experiences after settlement in each nation and consider the following questions: What kind of educational and employment opportunities would be available to them? How would the culture and social and political institutions impact their identities, experiences, and larger conceptions of social membership? How would they fit into the existing racial arrangements and hierarchies of the US and Germany? To what extent would their Iranian, or foreigner, background impact their everyday lives and feelings of social citizenship and belonging?

2

Guilty by Association

Iran, the US, and the Power of Global Politics

I introduced the question of how foreign policy and critical international events, like the 1979 Iranian Revolution and the 1980 hostage crisis, have influenced and shaped Iranians' early migration and settlement experiences in chapter 1. In this chapter, I focus on three specific events—the Iranian Revolution and hostage crisis, the 2010 international sanctions against Iran, and the Trump presidency—to illustrate the centrality of global political dynamics in the racialization and politicization of Iranians and their social marginalization. I also argue that the enduring discourse of Iran as a "terrorist-sponsoring nation"—accompanied by state and global policies that consider Iranian nationals and those in diaspora as potential threats to safety and security   is centrally tied to Iranians' experiences of marginality and racism. While Iranians are not representatives of the Iranian government, they are persistently racialized as being "hostage takers," as a part of an "Axis of Evil," and as originating from a "terrorist-sponsoring country" that harbors anti-American and anti-Western sentiment—a lingering image associated with the hostage crisis.[1]

With the election of Donald Trump, the relationship between the US and Iran became even more precarious and hostile, as illustrated by several immigration and travel policies that target Iranians inside and outside Iran. This includes the 2017 Muslim Ban, formally known as Executive Order 13769: Protecting the Nation from Foreign Terrorist Entry into the United States,[2] which singles out nationals from countries such as Iran, Syria, and Yemen and denies them entry into the US by means of tourism, education, or family-reunification visas.[3] This policy targets both Iranian American citizens who have visited Iran in the past five years as well as Iranians with EU citizenship. It has been reported that the Muslim Ban disproportionality affected Iranians, followed by Yemenis and Syrians. A report by a New York–based nonprofit, Documented, highlights that between 2016 and 2019 there was a 60 percent decrease in the issuing of visas to affected countries. In the case of Iranians, between January 2017 and July 2020 there were a total of 36,859 Iranian nationals who applied for a visa, and about 7,000 of those applications were approved.[4]

Foreign policy relations became even more uncertain with the decertification of the 2015 Iran Deal, also known as the Joint Comprehensive Plan of Action (JCPOA), by the Trump administration. The May 2018 withdrawal, from an agreement that took extensive negotiations starting in 2013[5] between Iran and the US, the UK, France, Germany, Russia, and China, and the reimposition of economic sanctions on Iran, effective November 5, 2018, drastically altered the trajectory[6] of diplomacy between Iran and the United States. Other instances where President Trump worsened this already fraught relationship were his speech at the United Nations General Assembly in late September 2018, where he called Iran "a leading sponsor of terrorism,"[7] and a November 20, 2018, statement that accused the Iranian government of being "the world's leading sponsor of terror," trying to destabilize Iraqi democracy by supporting Hezbollah and Bashar Assad in Syria, and bearing responsibility for "a bloody proxy war against Saudi Arabia in Yemen." The Trump administration also labeled Iran's Islamic Revolutionary Guard Corps (IRGC) a "foreign terrorist organization" on April 2019, accusing it of being "an active and enthusiastic participant in acts of terror," one that aids and supports terrorism in the broader region.[8] The administration stated that "the Middle East cannot be more peaceful and stable without the weakening of the IRGC."[9] On May 19, 2019, President Trump tweeted: "If Iran wants to fight, that will be the official end of Iran. Never threaten the US again!"[10] The escalation of tensions with Iran came to a climax when Donald Trump ordered the US military to kill Iran's most prominent military commander, Qasem Soleimani, on January 3, 2020, under the rationale of a supposed pending attack on US military bases in the region. Following this, some argued that the strike against Iran's military, naval standoffs,[11] and threats of war were directed at changing the government of Iran. It is undeniable that the events of the Trump era produced significant tensions and challenges to the possibility of diplomacy between the US and Iran.

The ways that foreign policy and critical international events racialize, politicize, and negatively affect the lives of Iranians is well documented in both waves of interview data from 2010–2011 and 2016–2018. It is the follow-up interviews that show a clear shift in Iranians' narrations about their experiences in the United States. In contrast to the optimism of the 2011 interviews and the unbridled belief in the so-called American dream, Donald Trump's ascent to the presidency altered how some Iranians viewed American society. In the follow-up interviews, Iranians expressed an increasing sense of insecurity, fear, and doubt about their place in the US. Some felt that America's current discourse and policy toward Iran was reminiscent of the hostage crisis and that it had reawakened memories of trauma, marginality, racial profiling, harassment, and discrimination. While Iran-US relations had not been positive in decades and increased economic sanctions had been levied against Iran around the time of the 2010–2011 interviews, Iranians' experiences of marginality and racial and political stigma were less intense during the Obama era. For example, policies related to immigration and travel, work, and student visas did not profile Iranians—or disadvantage them—like they did once Trump took office. The Obama administration was also seen as being more willing to engage and build diplomatic relations with Iran, as would be seen later with the start of the Iran Deal negotiations in the 2013.

In what follows, I describe how geopolitical arrangements affect the lives of Iranians in the US by examining their experiences in the early 1980s, a time when anti-Iranian racism was palpable and Iranians experienced significant levels of discrimination and surveillance. This racism was mainstream and affected many aspects of life—from school to the workplace. Then I turn toward the twenty-first century and focus on the Iranian uranium enrichment program and the ramping up of international sanctions against Iran in 2010 to highlight how Iran's image as a "nuclear weapons–seeking," "terrorist-sponsoring" nation is reflected in the lives of Iranians. Lastly, I will show that the presidency of Donald Trump was a great concern for Iranians; they became increasingly worried about their place in the US and a potential war with Iran. A heightened sense of racial and political stigma and the reemergence of racial trauma and marginality were especially acute for first-generation Iranians; they told me that it was reminiscent of the hostile climate they experienced during the hostage crisis and the early 1980s.

The 1979 Iranian Revolution and 1980 Hostage Crisis

As I began to show in the previous chapter, Iranians living in the US were affected by the severing of US-Iran relations in several ways; they were bullied at school, experienced workplace discrimination, were threatened with or became targets of violence, and encountered surveillance and visa problems, including deportation. To highlight how widespread marginality was, and the implications this would have on Iranian identity and community, I begin with those who were adolescents during the hostage crisis, then move to international students at American colleges and universities, and then turn toward Iranians' workplace experiences. This array of experiences demonstrates the power of foreign policy relations in facilitating the production of social marginality—seemingly overnight.

Hostage Takers

Iranians who were adolescents and going to school during the hostage crisis described a climate in which anti-Iranian racism was widespread. Nader migrated in the late 1970s when he was eleven years old with his family to the southern part of the Bay Area. He recounted his early experiences at school:

> NADER: I was not well received . . . having an accent and having to
> experience some of that. And after two years came the hostage
> crisis. By that time, I was in high school. By then I had lost most
> of my accent, but I did get a lot of attention and there were people
> that wanted to beat me up. I hated it, and I felt like I had to hide my
> identity somewhat, so I wasn't really forward with the fact that I was
> Iranian.
> S: Did you adopt a different name in high school?
> NADER: Yes, I went with Ben. That was one of the first things that my
> and I cousin did; we picked an English name so that we could fit in.

The hiding of identity, not wanting to be forthright about background/ancestry, and feeling shame around being Iranian were common among Iranians who were adolescents during this period. Nader and his cousin felt the need to hide their background and quickly learned that adopting an English name could protect them from bullying and physical harm. The name change could not, however, alter their phenotype, racial/ethnic background, or connection to an Iranian homeland; Nader remained hypervisible at school and a target of racial bullying and violence. He went on to describe how his decision to play football in high school was an attempt to fit into American culture and hopefully gain the acceptance of his peers:

> In high school, I started playing American football. I did it somewhat to
> fit in; it was an easy way to get acceptance. And of course, it was tough
> playing American football for an Iranian, because we barely had any real
> PE programs and were not familiar with rough sports like football. First
> year was kind of tough, because I was smaller and younger than the others, but by the second season I was better. After you get hit a bunch of
> times, you get tougher, you sort of earn your respect and place from your

team. Once you get on good terms with your team, it gets easier. . . . If you look at African Americans, it was also through sports that they were accepted; being a part of that allowed them to be more accepted by white society.

Nader's point about race, gender, and sports is telling and illustrates something revealing about American society. First, young boys and men seem to only be able to gain the respect of their peers—and possibly decrease racism—through physical toughness.[12] By being on the team and becoming good at an all-American sport, like football, you may be able to enter the group. Second, America has a history of racism and exclusion; Black people, for example, have also had "to prove themselves" to make gains in white society, and in many cases that was achieved through excellence in sports. Nader later named a few Black and Mexican classmates and fellow football players as having been accepting of him and later becoming some of his closest friends in school. He also compared his experiences to those of other racialized people when he went on to describe how his Mexican teammate "had it even worse than me with all the 'wetback' jokes," and thus maybe "Iranians did not have it as bad as others." Nader's experiences point to several important issues. One is that global political events, like the hostage crisis, were powerful in facilitating racialization and the production of social marginality. Second, he also details the attempts and mechanisms employed to ameliorate marginality and racism, including the role of racial/ethnic friendship[13] in providing some refuge and relief from racist experiences. Nader was one of the interlocutors who critiqued the view of the US as "a nation of immigrants," stating that "some Americans are 'free-er' than others." It was his first-hand experiences with prejudice and racism that had ultimately informed his political orientations and views of US society.

As I began to show in the previous chapter, international students in the US were especially vulnerable to the hostile social climate, given that many had migrated alone, and few Iranian American organizations existed at the time. Tony, a first-generation professional living in the Bay Area, described the climate in Mississippi when he arrived from Iran in 1979 to study engineering as a PhD student:

> Some of the Middle Eastern groups put up signs that read "I am not Iranian" and they got beat anyway, they'd say, "You're lying, you are from there." But we did not go out, we only went places we knew.

He also recalled public harassment and incidents of racial profiling:

> I recall one time I was sitting at an indoor shopping mall with two of my cousins and then this undercover guard comes over and said, "Can I see your ID?" I said, "No, you can't. Who are you?" He said, "I am undercover, sir." I said, "Okay, show me your badge," So he shows me his badge. "So what is the problem? I am just sitting here." He said, "No, but if I see you doing something then it's going to be trouble." He was trying to threaten us; they were rednecks, they didn't know any better.

The climate across the US was deeply racist for Middle Easterners and Muslims and being surveilled and treated with suspicion was common. Vigilante behavior and racism from ordinary white Americans were more frequent than in previous years. Tony states that the racism was considerable and other groups responded to this climate by placing signs on their windows declaring their non-Iranian background. While he did not think that saved them from harassment, we would see this method repeated twenty years later when Iranians would place signs on their businesses after 9/11 stating that they were not Arabs. Tony and other Iranians responded to rising anti-Iranian racism by either not going out, or only going to places they were familiar with. Unfortunately for Nick, who was attending the University of Seattle, going to places he was familiar with and "being careful" did not guarantee his safety. He went on to describe an incident in which he was a target of violence:

One night we went to this hamburger spot in Seattle; it was a very popular place. We were speaking in Farsi and this guy grabbed me from behind and choked me, screaming, "Let my people go!" I couldn't breathe. I went unconscious, and when I opened my eyes, there was an ambulance, the police, the guy in handcuffs, and one of our friends was crying, he was devastated. The police asked me what happened, and I said that "we were speaking in Farsi" and that he grabbed me, choking me, saying, "Let my people go." I said, "I have nothing to do with your people. I'm just like you." We went to gas stations, and they would not give us gas. It was bad. So, after that, we didn't go out at night. If we did go out, we spoke in English. We went through a lot of stuff.

Vigilante behavior on the part of white Americans and rising nativism had increased racial violence toward Iranians—and anyone suspected of being Iranian. While the racialization of Muslims and people from the Middle East had existed prior to this, the Iranian Revolution and hostage crisis ushered in a new era of demonization. For Nick this racism led to violence and physical harm. The widespread negative representation and portrayal of Iran and Iranians in American TV is well documented.[14] The portrayal of Iranians as "hostage takers" deeply impacted the American psyche and facilitated a climate in which ordinary white Americans felt compelled to attack Iranians, both verbally and physically. The sentiment against Iranians was so intense that they were attacked in public spaces and were refused services and goods. These mostly young Iranians felt stuck and traumatized in many ways. One the one hand, they could not or would not return to Iran because they were opposed to what was happening, and on the other hand they were being attacked and mistreated in the nation they assumed would provide them refuge, a new start. They were also separated from their families, not knowing when they would see them again. These experiences have undoubtedly left a deep mark on the memories and experiences of Iranians in the US; the hostage crisis years continue to be a traumatic subject for the Iranians who lived through them.

Rising anti-Iranian prejudice and racism had also made the work-place more difficult to navigate. Iranians saw their relationships and interactions with coworkers and supervisors change overnight. Surveillance and discrimination ensued. Dawn, a second-generation Iranian who was born and raised in Los Angeles, spoke about her parents' work experiences during the 1980s:

> During the hostage crisis and revolution, my dad worked for a government agency, and basically, they started an FBI file on him. They brought him in and started asking what his ties were and what was going on. He was treated so unfairly. Even when he worked for a private company, he had problems with coworkers or superiors who were typically white and typically religious Christians. Talking about religion and ethnicity in the workplace and being very inappropriate and discriminatory.

During and after the hostage crisis, Iranians were increasingly racialized as "dangerous others" and "hostage takers" discriminated in educational institutions, the workplace, and public spaces. Iranians were frequently associated with the Iranian government and its actions, and consequently intimidated and profiled. Those working for American government agencies were suspected of working for or being tied to the Iranian government; unfounded suspicion over their committing espionage ensued. Iranians, like Dawn's father, experienced workplace discrimination in both the public and private sector. Ironically, so many of these Iranians were ultra-opposed to the newly established Iranian government and wished for its destruction daily. So for Iranians in the US to be associated with Iran's policies and actions when they themselves left—and have not returned—is peculiar and nonsensical.

While a few years prior Iranians spoke of access to educational and work opportunities, by the early 1980s they were racialized as "hostage takers" and had become "enemies of the state" and associated with a "fundamentalist, Islamist" homeland. This shift in the social and political climate and the explicit vilification of Iranians in American mainstream society influenced and shaped the personal and public lives of Iranians along with their economic opportunities. Analysis of US media coverage of Iran outlines how Iranians have been depicted among different administrations: as "hostage takers" during the Carter administration, as "barbarians" during the reign of Reagan, and as being a part of an "Axis of Evil" during the George W. Bush years. The experiences of the interlocutors illustrate how changing political alliances and relationships and discourse pose significant consequences for those associated with a vilified Iran.

The Iranian Uranium Enrichment Program, aka the Iranian Nuclear Program

The timing of the 2010–2011 fieldwork coincided with several important international decisions and policies directed at Iran, and Iranians spoke to me at length about Iran's uranium enrichment program and the additional sanctions that had been imposed. While the Iranian government insisted that their end goal was not to acquire nuclear weapons, the program further characterized Iran as a defiant nation that was unwilling to abide by the international communities' rules. The incessant political discourse about a "desire to acquire nuclear weapons" had amplified conversations about Iran being a "sponsor of terror" and placed Iran in the American and global spotlight once again, elevating the anxieties of Iranians.[15]

Sponsors of Terror

The additional sanctions heightened the portrayals of Iran as a dangerous nation that had gone "rogue." In the span of thirty years, Iran—and by extension Iranians—have gone from "hostage takers" to being a part of the "Axis of Evil," and more recently to "sponsors of terrorism." Bez, a first-generation man living in southern California who had moved to the US as an adolescent in the early 1980s, described the role of the media in the portrayal of Iran:

Iran is seen as a snotty little kid who doesn't listen and that won't get in line. It's funny because you see these headlines and it's never objective. You can have two headlines: Iran has issues with the current UN inspections teams and halts inspections until another team is put together, or you can say Iran remains defiant. You know each headline is different. If you're living in Middle America, which headline are you more likely to believe? Well, that's how most countries see Iran.

Western media depicts Iran as a defiant nation, one that moves against the rules and norms of the international community by its commitment to developing a nuclear program. Bez argues that while a more nuanced and complex story about a nation's right to uranium enrichment could be told, media coverage about Iran remains biased. These portrayals are not without implication or consequence—they shape public opinion about Iranians and foreign policy about Iran. Bez went on to tell me that Iran has a right to enrich uranium and that it does not pose a danger to other countries in the region. He believed that the targeting of Iran was rooted in the US still not being over the revolution; "they have scores they want to settle with Iran." Not granting Iran admittance into "their political community" was ultimately about Iran not having power in the region.

The sanctions also generated another layer of suspicion around the identities of Iranians in the US and further associated them with a nation that "will not get in line." Iranians stressed the centrality of Iran's global political reputation and position in shaping their ability to secure resources and climb the mobility ladder in the US. Maryam, a first-generation immigrant woman living in southern California, described the US as a place of ample opportunity and a "nation of immigrants." She had received a bachelor of science and a master's degree at a California state university, was employed as a nurse when we spoke in 2011, and was generally satisfied with her life in the US. Despite these positive experiences, she described how Iran's relationship with the US has affected the academic and economic lives of ordinary Iranians:

I think that entering the job market may be difficult or a challenge. To continue education in some ways, let's say a person is Iranian and the other person is American, naturally the American will be chosen. Even though the Iranian is more qualified. So it's not without effect, because the minds of people are filled with the media. Whether you want it or not, the media and propaganda is in people's heads, and it affects various aspects of one's lives, work, education. Even living in an environment where everyone is American may make one uncomfortable.

She also finds that negative media portrayals of Iran and the Middle East are powerful and shape how Iranians are seen and treated in school, at work, and in public. These images are a form of propaganda; they fill the minds of Americans with the idea that Iranians are dangerous people that should be watched. Maryam contends that this kind of image of Iranians, which is the dominant one that is promoted in the media, inevitably impacts the professional opportunities of Iranians. If an employer had to choose between an Iranian and a white American job candidate, the latter will get the position. Pointedly, she references the type of racial aggressions that Iranians may experience by commenting about "being uncomfortable when living in a neighborhood where everyone is American." In this context, Maryam is referring to white Americans when she uses the term "American," and it is often white Americans who are named as being the primary source of hostility, discomfort, and marginalization for Iranians compared to other racial/ethnic groups in the US. Ultimately, she believed that while she had been able to create a degree of comfort in the US, the lingering and persistent hum of the US's relationship was always there, and one "had to pay a price for being Iranian in America."

Clearly, the negative assumptions and depictions of Iranians present significant challenges in the securing of higher-level professional opportunities. Cyrus, whose migration story I shared in the previous chapter, said the following about employment in the US, especially in the field of science and technology:

There are lots of people of Chinese background, a lot of Vietnamese, but not that many Iranians. I think Iranians are to some degree being watched. They are an issue, and this affects the job situation. Any kind of technology is knowledge. They don't want that knowledge to be given to Iranians . . . the challenge for Iranians is to not be limited. So Iranians being the people that they are, they are very proud, and really want to do their own thing, so they become doctors so that they can be in control of their own practice, so that they don't have a boss. Or they become a lawyer, or they have their own business. It's about being independent, because the society is very, very hostile toward Iranians. It's a very hostile situation here, and this is not the time for Iranians to really grow with the government.

Cyrus has had a significant amount of educational and professional experiences in the US since arriving for his PhD. He had lived in the US long enough to experience the climate before the revolution and after. He had also attained a good quality of life for himself and his family, yet professional or financial success did not mean that he had not experienced discrimination or racism in the workplace. He felt the impact of sanctions professionally and believed that they had made Iranians more prone to marginalization and being disadvantaged in the labor market. Suspicion of Iranians meant that they had more difficulties in working in fields such as information technology, aerospace, and intelligence gathering. Cyrus suggested that Chinese or Vietnamese workers were preferred over Iranians because of the perception that they were more loyal to the US. It was assumed that Iranians would leak sensitive information to the Iranian government because their allegiance is to the Iranian government. Of course these stereotypes are not unheard of; one only has to look at the treatment of Japanese Americans during World War II as evidence of American citizens being accused of espionage because of their racial/ethnic ancestry or at the post-9/11 climate in the US where the civil rights of American citizens were routinely violated because of their religious faith.[16] For Cyrus, the assumptions made about Iranians produce a climate in which they experience more discrimination in the labor market, making it especially difficult to secure federal employment. Iranians who have the financial resources, in turn, often respond to this persistent racialization by becoming "their own boss." The establishment of a private business or private practice makes it feasible to attain a good quality of life, curtail or bypass experiences of discrimination and racism, and preserve pride and dignity. In this context, the practice of entrepreneurship becomes a means of coping with racial/ethnic marginality and labor market discrimination.

The new sanctions[17] passed against Iran by the UN Security Council would also toughen "rules on financial transactions with Iranian banks and increase the number of Iranian individuals and companies that are targeted with asset freezes and travel bans."[18] This meant that Iranian Americans could no longer conduct business in Iran, buy property, or transfer money internationally, and were central in decreasing Iran's business relationships with the global community. The additional 2010 sanctions further complicated the use of third-party money transfer systems. While it is legal for ordinary Iranians to send remittances to their families in Iran, some have been caught in the cross hairs of the ambiguity of the law.[19] Those who visited family in Iran on a regular basis or financially supported their families were especially concerned about the ramifications of these fresh sanctions. For example, Aref, a second-generation Iranian American lawyer from northern California, described how the sanctions had affected the business relations and property investments of Iranian Americans in Iran:

> The sanctions that have been in place against Iran are completely unreasonable, they have been, and they know . . . they know. . . . I had someone who left the United States with half a million dollars. They wanted to buy an apartment in Iran, and you must report that level of income coming out. And when they asked, and he said, "I'm buying a house," "You're not supposed to do that." What are you going to do? "I'm buying a house in the country where I lived." That's an unreasonable thing to say. I was

in Iran, and I had all my accounts frozen here because I was physically there . . . it was a rule.

Under the most recent round of economic sanctions, purchasing property in Iran, maintaining a business partnership in Iran, even sending money to family in Iran was virtually impossible. The economic sanctions also impacted those who had traveled to Iran for tourism or to visit family; as Aref stated, being "physically" in Iran could cause one's American bank accounts to be frozen or closed.

Since the 2000s, Iran has been persistently depicted as being a part of an "Axis of Evil," a nation bent on acquiring nuclear weapons, and Iranians have born the burden of these accusations. They have been suspected of being disloyal to the US—despite their US citizenship—and their opportunities for advancement, especially employment with state institutions and agencies, are limited. US-Iran relations are central to their experiences of marginality and racial othering. Naturally, then, many believed that better relations between the countries would benefit Iranians in diaspora. If things improved between the nations they could travel to and from Iran with more ease, economic relations would improve, and owning property or supporting family in Iran would be simpler. Lastly, if Iran was cast in a better light in the US and globally, then Iranian Americans would be seen more positively too. Iranians often made remarks like "It may not go back to the times of the shah, but at least we'll be viewed better than we are now." Despite the ups and downs of the past decades, the Iranian interlocutors that participated in this research held out some hope that relations between the nations would have to get better one day.

The Trump Presidency

The presidency of Donald Trump sent shock waves throughout many communities across the nation, especially minority and immigrant ones. His election had changed some of the previously held assumptions that

Iranians had about the US and the larger American populace. Some told me: "This isn't the America that I love. This is not what this country is built upon." They argued that his election had shown immigrant and minority communities the ugly and racist side of this country. Moreover, they believed that anti-Iranian, anti-immigrant, and anti-Muslim racism was on the rise and would not disappear anytime soon. This was a sharp contrast from the more positive—even idealistic—views that Iranian Americans expressed in the 2010–2011 interviews.

It's important to note that there were also Iranians who supported Donald Trump, mostly because they had been against the Iran Deal and negotiations with the Iranian government. This group of Iranians insisted that the Iranian government had hoodwinked Obama and that the lifting of sanctions would not help ordinary Iranians, that only the powerful in Iran would benefit. These Iranians had not visited Iran for decades and had no immediate family in Iran; this could help explain their support for military action against Iran and their view that economic sanctions were necessary. They also told me that they would not set foot in Iran until the current Iranian government is changed. For this segment of the Iranian community, the Iranian government is not trustworthy and "one must play hardball with them." They believed that the deal had enabled the Iranian government to continue to "repress the Iranian people and cause conflict in the region." This set of Iranians also believed that Trump's promise to secure the US-Mexico border was necessary and long overdue. Like their white conservative counterparts, they felt that the "border was out of control" and that something needed to be done about "the illegal immigrants." They also viewed themselves as highly integrated in American society, and their economic interests seemed to also align with the Trump administration. I think it is interesting to consider that even their national politics and views about the US and whom they support are still being influenced by Iran and the global politics associated with it. Iran still played a central role in their political views and orientations, after all these years, even when they do not want it to. Notably, I encountered such remarks in my fieldwork in southern California[20] more often than in the Bay Area.

The following analyses are focused on how the election of Donald Trump has affected the lives of Iranians. I consider what the Iran Deal meant to Iranians in the US and how it impacted them, the way the Muslim Ban heightened anxiety and fear and further racialized and politicized the Iranian American community. I also explore how the negotiations for the Iran Deal were seen as creating a possibility for an improved relationship between the US and Iran. The Iran Deal was nonexistent when I conducted the 2010–2011 fieldwork, but it was a critical policy toward Iran, a step toward more positive political relations, and important to capture how Iranians felt about it in the follow-up interviews.

The Iran Deal

I asked a few open-ended questions about the Iran Deal that was officially signed in 2015. There was a general preoccupation with Trump and many of the interlocutors were already exhausted by the presidency only one year in. They considered the Obama presidency and the Iran Deal a distant memory. When I asked about the signing of the agreement in 2015, Mahrokh, an Iranian woman in her early thirties who had migrated with her family to the US as a child, described it as:

> A feeling of easiness, like it's not going to feel as constrained, like a general thawing, a sense that things are going to get easier. For a while—now that I think about it—like I really wanted to go to Iran, I was thinking about going by myself or even being there for a longer amount of time, and my mom, especially, had a lot of negative feelings toward that. "You don't know what it's like there, you are a single woman, what are you going to do there? I don't want you to get in trouble." She had a lot of scared feelings about that. But in the last two years, I think things have eased a bit and I think a part of that is

because it's being perceived that "oh, this relationship between the US and Iran isn't that bad, it's okay, things are easing."

Now that this weight had been lifted, Iranians could think differently about Iran-US relations. Mahrokh described an environment that is hopefully less intense and less complicated; she referred to it as an "easing and thawing" multiple times. She points out that Iranians, like herself, have often been dissuaded from going to Iran, especially alone. There had been a persistent discourse of Iran being a "dangerous place for single women."[21] Negative depictions of Iranians do not just impact non-Iranians; Iranians have also internalized some inaccurate portrayals and stereotypes of contemporary Iranian society. While many Iranians traveled from the US and across Europe to Iran every year without issue, the assertion that contemporary Iran is unsafe is common among Iranians, especially first-generation Iranian Americans. The Iran Deal is an example of an international policy that had the power to shift perceptions of both Iran and the Iranian people, as well as Iranians' perceptions of "ease and safety," encouraging some to visit Iran. Mahrokh, her father, and sister visited Iran together shortly after the deal was signed and reunited with their family in Iran after years of not seeing each other.

Many Iranians were especially concerned with how sanctions had created economic hardships for ordinary Iranians; some even considered economic sanctions to be a form of warfare. They told me that the deal was critical for the mending and improving of economic relations between the US and Iran and the larger global community, Nick discussed how he saw the Iran Deal impacting the lives of everyday Iranians:

To me as an Iranian and an American, I have spent more time here than there. I have been there three times in the last forty-two years. I think it was a good deal, for the people of Iran, because I could feel them, their excitement. I would see videos on YouTube—people looked like they felt that they would have more freedoms, they could do more things.

I asked what things specifically it would improve.

> It would mostly be economic. I talked to my mother this morning, and she said with your new US president, everything is more expensive now. All these things have greatly impacted the Iranian people. . . . Look at the Iranian currency; it's unstable, constantly going up and down.

Nick's discussion of the rising cost of food and goods is substantiated by reports citing economic recession and inflation and the suffering of ordinary people.[22] The Iranian currency continues to lose value and many Iranians are unable to purchase everyday items.[23] Sanctions had also created a medical crisis in Iran; medicine and medical treatment had become exponentially more expensive and difficult to attain. The pharmaceutical industry in Iran had been crippled by the sanctions leading to massive shortages of life-saving medicines.[24] Importantly, Iranians repeatedly told me that they did not see the Iran Deal as aiming to change the current government of Iran; it was a step toward diplomacy, and a way for those outside of Iran to be able to reconnect with those in Iran and vice versa. There was a possibility that the deal would cast a better light on Iran and by extension Iranians in diaspora. This hope of diplomacy and the lifting of sanctions came to an end when Donald Trump decertified the deal in May 2018.

The Muslim Ban

On January 27, 2017, Donald Trump signed Executive Order 13769: Protecting the Nation from Foreign Terrorist Entry into the United States, also known as the Muslim Ban. It became effective the following day and targeted foreign nationals from seven predominately Muslim countries, one of which was Iran. There was a range in how the Muslim Ban impacted Iranians in the US. Some had witnessed the cancelation and denial of their friend and families' student, business, and travel visas.

Others had family in Iran cut off from vital medicine and medical treatment. My conversations with Iranians in the summers of 2017, 2018, and 2019 provided further insight into how the Muslim Ban separated fiancées and spouses; some were in the US while their spouse was visiting family during the passing of the Muslin Ban and unable to leave Iran. There were also Iranian families in Iran who had their US visa applications cancelled and were told that they had to start the process from the beginning—Mahrokh had close family members who experienced this. There were also international university students who were forced to stop their university studies because their parents were no longer able to financially support them because of economic sanctions and the continuous decline of the Iranian economy. Many found themselves working in Iranian restaurants, cafes, and grocery stores to save up money to hopefully go back to school, worried that their student visas would run out if they did not register for classes soon.

Soraya, a first-generation Iranian professional in her early forties who had migrated to southern California with her family at the age of thirteen, said this about how Iranians in Los Angeles perceived the ban:

I think everyone was offended. I think Iranians were offended to be included in that group. They really felt like the work that we have done, the contributions, we have already proven ourselves to be "different," and they were very offended to be included in that group. But it's also the first time, I live really close to LAX, and it's the first time I felt I could see Iranians putting their Iranian identity out there, because a huge part of what happens in LA is that you're Persian, you try to pretend like, you disassociate yourself. And suddenly people were like, "No! I'm Iranian. What are you doing? This is not okay." I think there was a shift, again maybe it's just my perception, but I think there was shift, where for the first-time people were like, they were like, "Oh, wait a minute, maybe they don't see us as accepted, as a part of this place." Because Iranians try to be model immigrants, like if we are highly educated, if we are contributing, if we are successful, then we are wanted, we will be seen as different, not like the other immigrants. I think it was a real shock for people to think that "oh my God, this is how they have grouped me?"

Iranians, or Persians, in Los Angeles were offended because they consider themselves to be a highly educated and financially success-ful immigrant group.[25] Iranians feel themselves to be well integrated and have made many efforts to become "model minorities" in the US. Iranians, especially those in LA, had contributed a lot to American soci-ety, and being singled out by Trump for their Iranian ancestry was both shocking and offensive. Soraya's assertion that Iranians were deeply upset and affected by the ban was supported by my conversations with other Iranians in southern California, as well as news stories across the nation.[26] Soraya also points toward the possibility of a shift in con-sciousness among Iranians; some had begun to question whether they truly belonged in the US. Relatedly, Mahrokh said this about the post-election climate and the Muslim Ban:

> The ban, to a certain degree, hit me way harder; that was a really, really, rough time. It was the first time, in a long time, where I felt unsafe, where I felt like I was being attacked. I have felt things that I later understood to be micro-aggressions, but this was one of the first times in a very long time where I felt completely unsafe. And here I am with fucking citizen-ship; there is no reason for me to feel unsafe.

Many regarded the ban as an insult and direct attack upon the Iranian American community. Iranians were upset that they were singled out in an immigration policy steeped in racism and Islamophobic ideol-ogy, especially given that Iranians had not committed any known acts of terrorism. For Mahrokh, the ban made her feel extremely unsafe; she questioned Iranians' place in the US. Her comment "and here I am a fucking citizen" points toward this sense that being an American citi-zen "should" protect her, but that her racial/ethnic background does not afford her that protection. She went on to comment on how the ban was impacting her family members in Iran as well:

> I had family members who were waiting for a visa to come, I had family members running into issues at the airport, I have a cousin in limbo because she is here on a student visa, and now she does not know what she will do. Yeah, so, I remember where I had this conversation with my dad where he said you should be careful with what you say and whom you say it to, and I remember thinking, "No. What? That's not how it was supposed to be." And my parents said things like: "We need to be more careful, because we don't know who is going to be able to come, or what if people start disappearing." So I was a mess.

Mahrokh had family members in the process of attaining a visa and it was unclear whether those who had visas previously approved would be allowed to come to the US. There were also Iranian international students across the US, like her cousin, who were unsure of whether they would be able to continue their studies. While Mahrokh had felt relief that Iran-US relations would improve just a few months prior and had even traveled to Iran after more than two decades, she was now increasingly worried. Her father even advised her to be careful "about what she said and did." The Muslim Ban reawakened Iranians' prior experiences and memories of political displacement and trauma, especially as it pertains to apprehension and "disappearance." Images and news articles of Iranians not being permitted to board planes to the US or being detained and questioned for hours at the airport by TSA and Homeland Security agents increased anxiety and a fear that Iranians were not safe in the US.[27] First-generation Iranian Americans were especially worried about the course of events.

As mentioned by Mahrokh, the Muslim Ban complicated the lives of many Iranians who were living in the US and those that had plans on coming. This also included Iranian international students studying in the US. My informal conversations with Iranians I met in 2017,

2018, and 2019 in Los Angeles underscored their fear of leaving the US with a student visa to visit family and not being able to not return. This was especially acute because of news reports and social media posts of Iranian students having difficulties returning to the US from Iran after winter break. I also spoke to Iranians who had come to the US during the Obama years and had been attending community and state colleges; with the increased sanctions and inflation in Iran, school had gotten too expensive, and they were forced to place their education on hold. At the time, they were working in various Iranian businesses until they could save up enough money to go back. Lastly, there were those who had separated from their fiancés and spouses due to the Muslin Ban and were still awaiting their return.

MAGA

Like Iranians' accounts of their experiences in the 1980s, the recent interviews also indicate how changes in the social and political climate are felt in the workplace. Nilou, a second-generation woman who practices law in southern California, talked at length about how the Donald Trump presidency had impacted her workplace environment. From the secretary who wore a pink MAGA hat while working the front desk to a clerk who challenged her about the president's social and political views, Nilou found that her work environment and some of the conversations and exchanges had changed—things had become more uncomfortable. She shared this encounter as an example:

> And then he made the statement, "I mean, I don't think he's a racist." And I was like, "Of course he's a racist. I would have more respect for you if you owned the fact that he's a racist and you're okay with it, that is different than saying I don't think he's a racist."

Nilou was caught in a conversation where a recently hired young clerk—a white male—was trying to get her to reveal her political views.

She told me that it felt like he was trying to get under her skin and aggravate her. She made repeated efforts to stop the conversation, but he persisted to challenge her about Trump. After she made her views clear, she told him that she was done arguing about Trump, because he was not going to be able to convince her that he was not a racist. He did finally leave her office, but Nilou had been surprised that he felt so emboldened to speak to her about politics at work. She explained that she felt tangible differences between the lawyers at the firm and the staff, including the clerks. According to Nilou, the lawyers were mostly liberal and progressive while the staff was mostly conservative. Importantly, she was also one of very few minority lawyers, so she felt especially uncomfortable with and irritated by having to "explain" her views on the current administration. She also believed that the social and political circumstances had given Trump supporters—like the secretary and the clerk—the freedom to "state their opinions." Essentially, they could make prejudiced and racist remarks because the president's rhetoric and policies had sanctioned it.

Donald Trump becoming president meant something very specific to Iranians; it was a sign that many white Americans must agree with his views of immigrants and non-white populations. His election symbolized a drastic shift away—in the exact opposite direction—from diplomacy toward Iran and the Iranian people. Siv had worked in the same dental office in northern California for the last sixteen years. She spoke of how the political focus on Iran had made things uncomfortable at work. Everyday conversations and exchanges had altered and not in a positive way:

At work, most of my colleagues are Republicans, and the doctor too. Sometimes I think it's just laughable; when we talk, I just keep saying, "This whole thing is ridiculous." In the first few days after Trump was elected, I was more upset, and I did try to stay out of it. When the patients would talk with the doctor, I would try to not get involved. Many times, when patients come in and are talking about Iran and the Middle East, they don't know where I'm from, maybe they think I'm South American. But the doctor tries to cut it right away; he will say, "Oh, Siv is from Iran. She can tell you about that." He changes the subject, so that they don't go there, so that they don't go any further with negative remarks.

Iranian Americans are persistently associated with Iran, and often stigmatized by the political relationship between the US and Iran. Siv works in an environment where she is aware that her employer and the patients have political views that are aligned with Trump and his administration. Moreover, the dentist—who is her employer—has often asked her to engage and directly answer the questions of the patients, because "being from there" makes her an "authority figure" on Iran. Siv also explained that Iranians are often forced into a position of either having to defend Iran—and by default the Iranian government—or they must demonize Iran. This, she told me, often places Iranians in sensitive and problematic situations at work and makes them prone to experiences of marginality and discrimination.

Will We Be Safe?

Iranians were also worried about their safety and the safety of their families, especially those in Iran. Many had older parents who had dual citizenship and frequently visited the US as well as family members who held dual citizenship in Europe and Iran. There was anxiety over what changes were in store for those of Iranian ancestry. Despite legal status and American citizenship, Iranians did not feel protected. Tony shared some of the problems he foresaw for Iranians with dual citizenship:[28]

> My sister lives in London and she has two kids; they have been UK citizens for many years, and they never traveled to Iran in the last seven, eight years. When they came here last June, they had to get a visa; they still had to get a visa to come here. It is because they are of Iranian ancestry. And I'm afraid that other countries will follow suit, because when the

US places restrictions others do follow, maybe European countries will start doing it too.

The Visa Waiver Program[29] allows those with EU citizenship to visit the US without having to apply for a visa. However, this clause was changed for Iranians by the Trump administration, which means that European citizens of Iranian ancestry are required to have a US visa before they can enter the US. The singling out of Iranians was explicit and Tony was worried that other countries, especially European ones, would follow suit and target Iranians in similar ways. Like Tony, Nick also cited several concerns regarding his family, specifically his mother who held both American and Iranian citizenship. She lived in Iran and annually traveled to Germany and the US to see her sons. This is how he describes the Muslim Ban impacting her visits:

> At first, she wanted to change her plans. The plan was to come here and then go to Germany together. She would stay for two and a half months. But then she said, "Are they going to bother me?" She was still hesitant, and I said, "If you think it's going to give you a heart attack, don't come here, go to Germany and I'll see you there." But my cousin in Tehran did a little bit of research and reassured her that she would be fine.

Nick's elderly mother who lived in Iran had US citizenship and visited him and his older brother once a year, but reports of Iranians being detained at airports left her and many others in a state of fear and anxiety. It was widely reported that even Iranians who were green card holders and US citizens had their plans delayed, were left stranded, or had been unable to board their connecting flights to the US. There were also numerous stories of Iranian permanent residents and citizens being questioned or detained for a prolonged amount of time shortly after the ban was declared. It is undeniable that US foreign policy toward Iran continues to make it difficult for Iranian families who live in different countries and regions to be able to see each other.

The changing social and political climate in the US and the explicitly hostile approach of the Trump administration's dealings with Iran had also made some Iranians question the limitations of US citizenship. Some wondered whether their American citizenship would keep Iranians safe. Since we had last spoken in 2011, Siv had become an American citizen, and in her 2017 follow-up interview she described what led her to that decision:

> It's about security and about protection from deportation. Being able to have more protection. It opened a lot of things for me. I was able to get an American passport and can travel with more ease. But because we are Iranian, we are always in fear; we've always had to be. That's what sets us apart from others. Look, it is really unfair. All these terroristic groups are from Saudi Arabia and Pakistan. All of them get trained there and then come and drop bombs. And then this idiot goes and dances with them and applauds them and shows support and friendship to them. But Iran is the one singled out in the policies.

Siv brings up a few important points about American citizenship, safety, perpetual fear, and the contradictions of US foreign policy toward Iran and the "war on terror." She explained that Iranians were a hyperpoliticized immigrant group in the US, and that this has caused many, including her, to live in fear and with a persistent sense of worry and anxiety. She cited "protection from deportation" as one of the main reasons for becoming a US citizen. She also mentioned that the US's ongoing relationship with Saudi nations and Pakistan is contradictory, because if the US was concerned with terrorism or the "war on terror," the economic and political relationships between the nations would have ended after 9/11. Her reference to Trump as an "idiot who dances with them" is meant to underscore that it is "idiotic" that the president of the US is dealing and trading with nations and governments that have engaged and continue to participate in terrorism. Siv, like other Iranians whom I spoke with, believes that the US's ongoing problem with Iran is not about Iran being "a terrorist-sponsoring" nation, but rather America's desire to change the current Iranian political establishment.

The follow-up interviews draw attention to the role that critical international events play in the lives of Iranians in the US and those in Iran. For Iranian Americans, the election of Donald Trump, the "Muslim Ban," and the decertification of the Iran Deal have all resulted in increased experiences of fear, danger, and marginality. Mahrokh, Nick, Siv, Soraya, and Tony all describe the many ways in which the passing of policies that ban Iranians from being able to come to the US for travel, work, or educational purposes is politically stigmatizing. Becoming an American citizen as a form of protection from deportation is a vivid manifestation of fear, stigma, and trauma. It is also not new; since the early 1980s Iranians have become US citizens as a means of protection because they have persistently felt the American social and political climate to be a danger to them. What is more, Iranians also believed Trump's rhetoric and policies that facilitated and emboldened white Americans to be explicitly racist.

The Reawakening of Past Marginality and Trauma

As shown, Iranians experienced anxiety and fear, felt that "things had changed at work," and their previous assumptions about belonging and membership were being challenged. These follow-up conversations not only demonstrate the relationship between social and political climate and sense of belonging, well-being, safety, and social membership. They also point toward the fragility of belonging for those with racialized and politicized identities; seemingly overnight, Iranians have found themselves in the center of geopolitical affairs—once again.

The election of Donald Trump and the Muslim Ban had reawakened a kind of trauma that Iranians experienced during the hostage crisis. The explicit anti-immigrant, anti-Muslim, and anti-Iranian rhetoric and policies of the Trump administration had aroused and ignited a form of racism that Iranians had either forgotten or not seen before. And many

Iranians felt the way Trump spoke and the anti-immigrant racism that he harbored had given his followers and ordinary white Americans a free pass to publicly express their racist beliefs. First-generation respondents who had been in the US in the late 1970s and early 1980s, especially in their adolescent, teenage, or young adult years, felt that they were reliving the traumatic experiences of their past. For example, Tony believed that history continues to repeat itself and that the position of Iranians in the US had not changed dramatically since he migrated in the 1970s. By "position" he did not mean economic position, but rather the assumptions that are made in the mainstream about Iran and Iranians. In our January 2017 follow-up interview, he went on to say:

> Now that the vampire can come out during the daytime, how will this impact Iranians? I'm afraid that for us, for Iranians, we may go back to the hostage crisis, those feelings, and experiences we had then. The negative experiences come alive; they are still doing the same things.

Those who had been in the US during the hostage crisis found the present social climate to be especially alarming and worrisome. Tony's sentiments were echoed throughout the follow-up conversations that I had with first-generation Iranian Americans, specifically that discourse and policy toward Iran was becoming increasingly worrisome, and this had negative ramifications for in Iran and those in diaspora. Moreover, in the words of Tony, the "vampire can come out during the daytime," meaning that racists are being allowed to publicly spew hateful and offensive remarks about Muslims and Middle Easterners without repercussion. Racism and prejudice have become explicitly acceptable in the US, and it was the president of the US that had sanctioned it. As shown in chapter 1, Tony's experiences of being an international PhD student in Mississippi during the hostage crisis were not positive; he had plenty of memories of anti-Iranian and anti-Muslim racism in the early 1980s. These past experiences coupled with the changing US climate had reawakened his fears of "Iranians being targeted once again." Nick also mentioned how the current climate reminded him of the hostage crisis when we spoke again in late 2018. He told me:

> It does. Because I was here, I was a student, I was going to college, and I came here in 1976 and it was 1979 when the revolution happened. I remember going to a gas station and the guy coming out with a shotgun and saying, "Get out of here! Get out of my country! You are taking over our oil!" and I said, "What do you mean I'm taking over your oil? I am a student here. I have nothing to do with oil or hostages." Because of the hostages, there was an oil embargo so there was not much oil coming into the US. I don't know if you remember, but there were lines for gas.

The hostage crisis remains a vivid reminder of anti-Iranian prejudice, racism, and discrimination. It was Nick who in his 2010 interview described an incident in which he was physically beaten in a hamburger place in Seattle for speaking Persian with friends during the hostage crisis. The racism that the Donald Trump presidency promoted brought up memories of living in fear and reminded Iranians that they were still not seen as real Americans, that they would continue to be racialized, and that white Americans felt emboldened to attack them. Nick went on to tell me of an encounter he had in the fall of 2017 that involved being verbally attacked for speaking Persian with a friend on public transportation (BART) in the Bay Area:

> I was on the BART to the SF airport to go to Seattle. . . . I was riding the BART with my friend. We were talking and this lady next to us—a white lady probably in her fifties—stood up and said, "You know you can't talk in that language." And I replied, "What language?" and she said, "Whatever language that you are talking." And I said, "You don't even have enough education to understand what language I'm talking, so why are you telling not to speak it? I can talk any language that I like, I'm not breaking any laws. This is my country, and I have probably been here as long as you." And then she starts, "No, Donald Trump says we should

always speak English." And I said, "Fuck you and Donald Trump, at the same time."

As in years prior, we see white Americans increasingly policing public space. Nick felt that the rhetoric and policies of the Trump administration had a direct bearing on the current racial and social climate of the US.[30] He was harassed on public transportation for speaking non-English in public, and this private citizen saw it as her responsibility to advocate for Donald Trump and his vision of making America "great again." This type of white vigilante behavior had convinced Nick that Iranians would be singled out and discriminated against, yet again. Regardless of being American citizens or how many years they had lived in the US, Iranians would bear the burden of nativist policies. Seemingly, Iranians are associated with negative portrayals of Iran no matter how "integrated they appear and behave" or how long they have worked or lived in the US. Like other Iranians, Nick blamed white Americans' lack of education and culture[31] for their prejudice and racism. Ultimately, when I asked Nick about how the past two years have impacted his everyday life in the US, he sadly stated:

> It's not a good feeling. Nowadays, I'm more careful when I go out. When I open my mouth. When I talk to somebody, if I'm with an Iranian, I watch the people around me. When we are speaking both Persian and English, I'm watching and looking for someone to come and say or do something to us. You don't know what's going to happen, how they will react.

Feelings of uncertainty, the need to cover or repress racial/ethnic background and "melt" into the larger population, were back. When the environment changes like this, Iranians' immediate reaction and response is to move "below the racial radar." This process entails not drawing attention to cultural and religious differences, not publicly displaying signs of being Iranian or Muslim, and avoiding conversations that are about Iran or the Middle East. In the 2017–2018 interviews, Iranians also indicated that feelings of anxiety and fear had reemerged as well as the sense that they had to "watch themselves" in public in ways that they did not express in 2010–2011. Nick's point that these events and encounters reminded him that "you are from somewhere else" are an illustration that no matter how long Iranians live in the US they have yet to be seen as Americans. That they "do not really belong here."

Nader, who was an adolescent during the hostage crisis, also spoke to me at length about things he had experienced in the past six years when I followed up with him in 2017. He told me that the nativist discourse and policies of the Trump administration had reawakened past experiences and painful memories of racism:

> It has made me unravel all this stuff from my own past [he starts tearing up]. This stuff is from so long ago, I've put it away, it's not something I actively think about, the negative experiences of being a preteen and teenager while all that stuff is going on. Being in a hostile environment, at a majority white school—it was not diversified, there was no political correctness back then; people were outright with their racism and views. All that was filed away. Now because people are being more open again with their racism, it's making me have flashbacks to how people were back then . . . hearing other people saying that someone said to them, "Go back to where you came from," I used to hear that all the time, it was always normalized [starts tearing up]. As an adult, I don't hear it anymore. But hearing other people point out that they were told that they don't belong here, that they don't have a right to be here, hearing other people recount their stuff makes me say, "Oh, I went through that. Oh, that happened to me" [starts tearing up again].

Trump's political platform and his anti-Muslim and anti-immigrant policies had brought back memories of Iranians being bullied in school, of feeling less than, and of feeling ashamed of their ethnic and religious background. Nader's[32] story was not rare among the Iranians

I spoke with in the follow-up interviews. Although I had heard many of these stories in 2010–2011, the way they recounted them now felt more intense, more emotional, and raw. It was indeed a sort of "vampire coming out in the daytime," so to speak. This reemergence speaks to the ebbs and flows of racial trauma and marginality. While these memories may not be bright or accessible every day—and while some may have been buried away—a social and political climate that promotes the "banning" of people from Muslim-majority nations, actively calls for the deportation of undocumented people, and makes white nationalist rhetoric mainstream has traumatic effects on minority and immigrant communities. Nader told me that it was being among a yoga group and training with mostly other immigrants and Black and brown people that created a space for him to be able to express these feelings and memories of racial marginality, trauma, and fear. It was in this space that he heard the stories of others and was able to better access memories of racial injuries and trauma. He had flashbacks of what the climate in the US felt like and was reminded of how badly Iranians, like himself, had been treated.

The stories of Nader, Nick, and Tony remind us that the past has not passed and that the racialization and politicization of Iranians is ongoing. A major consequence of this racialization is that Iranian Americans still do not feel fully sure about their place in American society and are uncertain about what the future holds. These shifts underscore the fickleness of belonging and social membership where one's status and treatment in society is often uncertain and not tied to one's own efforts. It also vividly highlights that racialization slows down and picks up alongside social and political climate, discourse, and policy. The rhetoric of Donald Trump and his administration is not without consequence—it is "bringing out the vampires," the racists, and facilitating the revival of explicit forms of white nationalism.

Discussion

This chapter has illustrated a few things. First, foreign policy and critical international events have had a considerable impact on the lives of Iranians in the past forty years. The political relationship between the US and Iran is central to Iranians' experiences of racialization and politicization, of marginality and discrimination. From the Iranian Revolution to the declaration that Iran was a part of an "Axis of Evil" by the Bush administration to international economic sanctions to the Muslim Ban and the decertification of the Iran Deal, Iranians in the US have been persistently racialized and stigmatized by global political affairs. The rise of nativistic discourse and policies that have singled out immigrant and minority communities also racialize and politicize Iranian and other non-white communities across the US. This has caused Iranians to question their place in the US, and even retriggered the negative and discriminatory ways that they were treated in the late 1970s and 1980s. There is a sense of uncertainty, of insecurity, and a feeling that Iranians may always be haunted by the relationship between Iran and the US. An "easing" is clearly not coming any time soon.

This chapter has also illustrated that economic success, social and cultural integration, US citizenship, and years of residence do not protect Iranian Americans from experiences of anti-Iranian prejudice and racism. Individual achievements, becoming "model minorities" through educational, professionals, or financial achievements and the adoption of American cultural norms and practices do not ameliorate the impact of global politics and critical international events. Even though Iranians are racially classified as white and may hold "honorary white status" in the larger racial stratification system, which puts them "above" other racialized people, they are not able to fully escape the ways that global political relations marginalize, racialize, and stigmatize them. They may be categorized as "racially white" by the US Census, hold "honorary white status," be American citizens, but often lack social citizenship. Moreover, the racial privileges they enjoy as members of a racially ambiguous community are liminal, temporary, and in flux. Maghbouleh's (2017) work on the limits of white racial classification for Iranian Americans is useful here. The experiences that I have detailed connect to what she calls *racial loopholes*, which consist of the "everyday contradictions and conflicts that emerge when a group's legal racial categorization is inconsistent with its on-the-ground experience of racialization or deracialization" (p. 5).

The racialization and political stigmatization of Iranians will persist for as long as the US and Iran continue to have a hostile political relationship, and for as long as the American government associates Iranians, Middle Easterners, and Muslim communities with "terrorism." Like decades past when the "Iran case" served a foundational and monumental role in presenting the "Islamic world" to a mainstream American audience, as argued by Said (1981), the "war on terror" is a continuation of the same story. A body of work has shown how the "war on terror" has greatly exacerbated the racialization of the identities of Arab, Muslim, and South Asians since 9/11 both in the US and abroad. This scholarship highlights how the racialization of Islam and Muslims are racial processes that are connected to larger US racial projects at home and abroad.[33]

The impact that this increased racialization has on belonging is clear; Iranians cannot feel safe, protected, or like equal members of society if they live in a state of perpetual alarm, anxiety, and fear. If anything, the current climate has reawakened past racial trauma and brought it to the surface. It has taught some, and reminded others, that the US is not a "land of immigrants" and that while their previously assumed ideas about American society were ideals to strive for, life in America was more complicated than they had known or assumed. It is not as "color-blind" as they had been taught to believe, and the educational and professional credentials and economic resources they had secured could not protect them from the marginality they had experienced. In chapter 4, I offer a deeper examination of the consequences of this persistent racialization and politicization on belonging and social membership. How can Iranians approximate "unconditional belonging" if they are perpetually associated with a country of rogue "hostage takers" that "sponsor terrorism?" How do they respond to, cope, and navigate experiences of racialization and marginality, and what can those mechanisms tell us about racialization and the larger racial systems of the US and Germany?

3

Refugees and *Ausländers*

The Persistence of Racial Nationalism

Unlike Iranians in the US who found themselves in the crosshairs of global political relations, Iranians in Germany were not conceived as "terrorists" or enemies of Germany but as refugees escaping persecution. The racialization and marginality that Iranians experience in Germany is less about Iranian-German relations and more about general anti-foreigner prejudice and the racism of German society. As outlined in chapter 1, Germany's self-conception is not rooted in being a "nation of immigrants," being "color-blind," racial/ethnic pluralism, or being a so-called melting pot. This means that those with non-German ancestry, or those with any family history of migration, are regarded as foreigners and treated as permanent guests despite having been in Germany for several generations.

Most non-Germans either arrived as refugees or guest workers in the postwar years. Between 1945 and 1949, around twelve million ethnic Germans who had previously been expelled and living in Poland, Czechoslovakia, Hungary, and Yugoslavia returned to Germany. These immigrants were able to integrate more easily given their German ancestry and the postwar economic boom. The second wave of migration occurred during Germany's recovery period. The bilateral labor recruitment agreement in 1955 between Italy and Germany was meant to fill labor shortages.[1] Similar guest worker agreements were made with Spain in 1960, Turkey in 1961, Portugal in 1964, and Yugoslavia in 1968. This second wave differed from the first in significant ways, specifically migrant ethnic background and guest status.[2]

The declining demand for foreign workers that began in 1973 led the German government to institute a ban on the recruitment of foreign workers; while some left, many former guest workers had attained residency and remained in Germany. Family reunification also increased the population of migrants despite the official curtailment of migrant workers. The rise of Muslim communities in Europe, including Germany, is mostly a result of postcolonial migration to former colonizing cities/regions through vigorous guest worker programs.[3] Continental Europe also experienced several geopolitical conflicts and crises in the late 1980s that caused a large influx of asylum seekers and refugees. Goldberg (2008) notes that while an aging European population increasingly needs refugees to work for the maintenance of the tax base, there is a growing view that Muslims, who tend to be hyperconcentrated in neighborhoods or urban centers, are "ethno-cultural polluters."[4] What is more, "renewed local fears of rapid demographic growth, 'swamping', and fears that European daughters will be 'lost to the veil of Islam and Muslim sons to the mania of terrorism' (p. 164) are reflected in public opinion polls throughout Europe (Goldberg 2008). These discourses, though, are not new—religious difference has long been used in theories of biological racism, as reflected in the ways that Muslims and Jews were essentialized and othered throughout the centuries across Europe.[5]

In this chapter, I consider how Germany's longer history of racial nationalism and anti-foreigner racism shape and influence how those racialized as *Ausländers* (foreigners) are treated throughout German institutions and broader society. I unpack the foreigner-native boundary by detailing how race-based conceptions of German identity show up in the construction of the derogatory term *Schwarzkopf*. This construct also presents itself when Iranians discuss the differences between "real vs. plastic Deutsch." I illustrate how being a foreigner in Germany—regardless of citizenship—comes with limitations and restrictions in higher education, vocational programs, and the labor market. The follow-up interviews I conducted in 2016 illustrate how these boundaries have become even more rigid since the 2015 refugee crisis. I point toward the events of New Year's Eve 2015 in Cologne as a point in time where the discourse around refugees drastically shifted and ruptured from the narrative of humanitarianism and became heavily focused on the "nature of the new refugees." Lastly, I consider how the rise of overt anti-foreigner racism and support for far-right political parties, like the Alternative for Germany (AfD),[6] have shifted racial boundaries and intensified racialization and experiences of threat, racial stigma, and "perpetual foreignness" among Iranians.

A Lasting and Lingering History

While twenty-first-century Germany is mostly regarded as a humanitarian, refugee-accepting society, a racialized conception of German national identity persists. Iranians often differentiate between German law and ordinary Germans. By law, Germany provides considerable support for asylum seekers compared to other European nations or the United States.[7] But in everyday life, Iranians experience ordinary Germans as maintaining anti-foreigner sentiment and prejudice. All the people I interviewed possessed permanent residency and the majority had a German passport, but this did not mean they felt like Germans or were always treated as equal members of German society. The conversations with second-generation Iranians demonstrated that being seen and accepted as German was rooted in culture and phenotype and that foreigners would never be German. They pointed to the differences between being "a German on paper" and being "a real German"[8] as examples of these race-based attributes and dimensions of German national identity and belonging.

Ausländer

According to the Statistisches Bundesamt (Destatis), foreigners who immigrated to Germany after 1949, those with foreign ancestry born in Germany, and all persons born in Germany with at least one parent who immigrated into Germany or was born a foreigner are classified as "persons with a migrant background."[9] Essentially, migrants remain foreigners or Ausländers[10] for three generations; those with foreign ancestry who are born in Germany or those who are born in Germany and have a German parent are not excluded from being classified as having a "migrant background." The German Census Bureau's official definition of "persons with a migrant background" emphasizes how descent-based definitions and criteria for membership continue to trump pluralistic or civil ones, and how German identity and national membership remain rooted in and framed by descent/race-based boundaries. Becoming a naturalized German does not change this. Moreover, as this chapter will show, phenotype and ancestry remain foundational to being "a German"; possessing citizenship does not erase racial/ethnic categories and distinctions.

I did not find much variation among first- and second-generation Iranians' descriptions of the German national context; while Germany accepts refugees, German people still struggle with seeing foreigners as being quite like them. There was also an underlying sentiment expressed to foreigners that they should be grateful they were granted refuge and that their basic needs were provided for by the state. Asking Germans for anything more was "asking for too much." Moreover, Iranians believed that Germans were still scared and suspicious of foreigners. First-generation Iranians who had migrated as young adults often provided nuanced views of German society. These were Iranians who considered themselves well integrated and relatively successful yet believed that Germans still maintained prejudice toward foreigners. Kimia, whose migration story I shared in chapter 1, told me this:

> Germans are not cold. They are scared. They are scared because it's strange to them. Germany has never been an immigrant nation, it became this way, but this has not resonated and settled in with them. We still have people who are alive from the World War II era, and I think this is something that I as a foreigner must understand. If I am using the opportunities here, they are not obliged to accept me, and I think many Iranians forget. Germans have no obligations or responsibilities for us. We have no inheritance or part of this place; we can try to integrate ourselves if we want to.

According to Kimia, Iranians and other migrant populations must confront and come to terms with several issues. First is that they are *Ausländers*, which means they must understand that they have no birthright or inheritance to Germany—this is not their homeland— they are long-term guests allowed to live there. The expectation that Germans will one day fully accept Iranians is "unrealistic." Second, Germans are not necessarily "cold" people—a common stereotype of Germans—rather they are "scared" and not used to living in a multicultural society. Older Germans, especially, are seen as harboring anti-foreigner prejudice and racism. Lastly, Kimia's assertion that "we can try to integrate ourselves if we want to, but we should not expect belonging" is tied to descent-based conceptions of social membership and belonging. Her comparison between Germany and the US is commonly made; oftentimes, the US is described as a society that "likes" immigrants compared to Germany, which is mandated to accept refugees. There was this implicit sentiment that America is a society that willingly accepts immigrants, while Germany is "forced to." Iranians in the US also made similar comparisons to defend the belief that America is more accepting of immigrants and non-whites than Europe, and hence a better society to live in. Pari, whose migration story I shared in the previous chapter, echoed some of Kimia's point and added that the fearful disposition toward foreigners was connected to race:

> Germans are fearful people; anything that is strange to them or unknown, they distance themselves from it. Only foreigners that they know—like the French, English, Sweden, Scandinavian countries, and Americans— can do well here. One reason is how people look; they are white like them. A Black American would be treated differently than a white American here. Anyone that's not a part of that racial group, they are suspicious of, and this bothers a lot of immigrants. This has bothered me a lot since I've been here. I've been in many terrible fights with Germans over this.

Pari argues that receiving a positive reception and doing well in Germany is racially rooted by citing the differential treatment that northern Europeans and white Americans receive in Germany compared to Black Americans and other racial/ethnic minorities. Like Kimia she also references "fear" and "suspicion" as the main reason for differential treatment, however she grounds this "fear" in racism. The racialization and marginality experienced is not about them being Iranian per say, it is Germany's longer history of racialization that deemed anyone that was not culturally and "biologically" German, and Christian, as people that should be feared and treated differently—that causes foreigners to be perceived as outsiders. Having lived in Germany since her early twenties had taught her that Germans treat people differently based on race. Iranians were also quite cognizant that length of residence or professional achievements would not lead to "unconditional belonging"; they knew that they lacked social citizenship despite having a German passport. Heide, whose story was highlighted in chapter 1, said the following about immigrants in Germany:

> No matter what you do you're still not German. No foreigner or non-German will say that they are German. In the US that's different, everyone calls themselves an American; you'll see a Chinese or Japanese person saying that they're an American. Someone may call himself or herself a German Iranian, but it's only to be politically correct, it's not really a reality. You will never become German.

Germany accepts refugees as people who need asylum, but it is not a "nation of immigrants" like the US. Germany is not a nation where a non-German immigrant can socially declare that they are "Iranian German"; it may be legally true and politically correct, but that is symbolic. The boundaries between Germans and foreigners remain racial; "you will never become German." Tellingly, the power of America's narrative of being a melting pot, a place where anyone can "become American" is illustrated in Heide's description of the differences between the US and Germany. In Germany, someone of non-German ancestry would not call themselves German, unlike non-whites in the US, who generally consider themselves to be "Americans" with different racial and ethnic backgrounds. In the US, being an American mostly denotes nationality, that one is a citizen of the nation. In Germany, being a citizen of the country does not mean non-Germans call or consider themselves to be "German." This distinction has much to do with the ways in which racial structure and hierarchies are constructed in various nations. In the post–Civil Rights era, there is a dominant narrative that belonging and mobility are not prohibited by race, ethnicity, or national origins in the US, but that they are achievement based and meritocratic, whereas in Germany ancestry is regarded to be a more powerful determinant of both mobility and social membership. The foreigner-native boundary[11] is racial and being a "foreigner" is code for being non-European, non-white, and being Muslim or identified as one. Being identified as a foreigner, an *Ausländer*, is a proxy for race. Obviously, Iranians feel constrained and believe that this racialization limits upward mobility and belonging. However, the expectation that Germans should view foreigners like themselves, and consider them equals, seems absurd to some of the Iranians I spoke with. They had been given the opportunity to live in a socially democratic nation and were provided with housing, healthcare, safety, and the opportunity to work and attend educational institutions. Expecting anything more, it is thought, is beyond the capabilities of Germans and German society.

Schwarzkopf

Ausländer is the German word for "foreigner," and is often used to describe someone with darker phenotypic features and someone who is culturally not Western and Christian. The term *Schwarzkopf* (literally, dark-haired person) is a derogatory version of *Ausländer* and a racial/ethnic slur that explicitly names darker features, such as skin tone and dark hair, and implies having ancestry in the larger Middle East and

North Africa. For example, Germans would not call a Polish immigrant a *Schwarzkopf.* I have vivid memories of this term being generously thrown around as a child, so when I asked Iranians about whether one's racial/ethnic phenotype mattered or carried weight in German society, it was not surprising to hear explicit mention of it. For example, when I asked Ismael, a second-generation Iranian man, if there had been any experiences at school that had made him feel different, he replied:

> Having dark hair, black hair, and knowing another language. I had more feelings of shame or being shy about some things. I noticed that I would feel ashamed about some things. My heritage, the language I spoke, and the things we did. And I noticed that this feeling changed when I came to Hamburg. So I had to hide it in Kiel, there were not that many other kids like me, but when we moved to Hamburg there were a lot more immigrants and foreigners in my classes.

The negative and stigmatizing connotations that being a black-haired foreigner—*Schwarzkopf*—carried are explicit in his experiences of marginality. Ismael names phenotypic and cultural differences as the source of his racialization. What had made him feel different than the other German kids at school was that he had dark hair and spoke Persian at home. He felt shame because of this and hid parts of his identity, including not using Persian in public, not taking Iranian food to school, and downplaying cultural differences. It would not be until his family migrated to a city with a significant foreign population that Ismael shed some of his shame and became more comfortable with being an Iranian and a foreigner. Importantly, we see the mention of friendships with kids of foreign background at school and in the larger neighborhood as ameliorating[12] feelings of shame and marginality.

Paul, also a second-generation Iranian and born and raised in Germany, spoke at length about both his and his father's experiences. He recounted being tracked at school and doing poorly academically and told me of his father's difficulties in the German labor market despite his German-language fluency and educational credentials. Paul was convinced that having foreign ancestry impacted professional and economic mobility. In response to my question about whether ancestry mattered in Germany, and to what extent, he told me:

> Yes, absolutely. I realized this when I was in grade school—the first four classes. I see it when I go out on weekends when people say, "You fucking foreigner." I have lived through things. I was with my friends, we were partying, and I was trying to get in, and they told me that "today, we're not letting foreigners in." You go there with your German friends to party, and they say that they can get in and you cannot. This shocks my friends, but you can't really say anything. That's how it is.

There was no question that phenotype mattered in how people were treated in Germany; this was especially acute in the experiences of foreign men. Iranian men spoke of persistent profiling and harassment in public spaces. From a young age they had learned that having darker features is what made them foreigners, and this was accompanied with a certain degree of disdain, loathing, and apathy toward them. The statement "you fucking foreigner" highlights how Iranians and those who are deemed "racially and culturally different" are singled out and harassed in public because of an unending racism and disdain that Germans maintain toward foreigners. Unlike his German friends who were seemingly surprised by the anti-foreigner racism, Paul was not. He was used to this treatment.[13] Similar to the narratives of first-generation Iranians, living in Germany had taught Paul to not expect anything more—"that's just how things are." This is quite different than second-generation Iranians in the US who often hold much more optimistic views about their place in American society. Kami, a second-generation college student, who had been raised in Germany since the age of five, further detailed the connotations and stereotypes of being a foreigner in Germany:

It seems to me that they don't care to distinguish, it's unimportant to know the differences between people—if they have dark hair, they must be from some of those regions. They have stereotypes, Muslim equals terrorist or they say that you're from a terrorist nation. It's more about being a foreigner, being from the Middle East, and specifically being Muslim . . . it's like if I were from Australia, they would say, "Oh, that's cool, you guys surf there?"

A central part of racialization[14] is the inscription of meanings and associations onto cultures, peoples, and regions; often these are negative, derogatory, and inaccurate. It also entails the erasure of national, ethnic, or cultural differences, and the lumping of a diverse group of people into one category. The belief that "all these people look the same," that they are "all *Ausländers*," speaks to the phenotypic component of racialization. Kami's view that "Germans do not care to know the differences" between various racial/ethnic groups speaks to this process. We also see how "a *Schwarzkopf*" is routinely associated with being Muslim, and being Muslim equates to either being a terrorist or coming from a terrorist-sponsoring nation. An Australian, as Kami points out, is not seen as a foreigner and is also associated with benign traits, such as surfing, compared to those coming from the larger Middle East, who are persistently linked to terrorism. The tropes and constructions encountered in Germany, across Europe, and in the US are similar because the racialization of Muslims and people from the Middle East is deeply rooted in ideas, images, and perceptions that the Western world has long held of the "Orient."[15] Notably, I did not come across a single Iranian who stated, in an unqualified manner, that one's racial/ethnic or religious background did not matter in Germany. All the Iranians I spoke with provided some follow-up or clarification of why background continues to matter in Germany.

Real versus Plastic Deutsch

It was not until January 2000 that Germany removed ancestry as the main criterion of attaining German citizenship.[16] However, having access to formal citizenship does not erase race-based conceptions of national identity. The race-based conceptions of "what a true German looks like" and "who a true German is" make it impossible for Iranians, and other migrant populations, to unequivocally see and feel themselves as part of Germany. It was telling that some Iranians explained how Germans viewed foreigners with German citizenship as "plastic Deutsch," as fake Germans, because German culture, identity, and belonging was inherent, essential, and based on ancestry or blood. "German-ness" could not be gained or achieved. The relationship between race and citizenship vividly appeared when I asked about citizenship and equality in ways that were not as blatant in the US interviews about citizenship. Paul said this about the citizenship:

> The passport doesn't say anything about being an actual German. On paper, I'm a German, but in reality I am an Iranian guy. I don't think that people around me think, "Oh, he looks like a German now, because he has a German passport." To that person, I am a foreigner.

Being German is about looking German, which means having "lighter" phenotypic features. Equal treatment is based on being an "actual German" and citizenship does not make you equal to native Germans. Phenotypically, Iranians still look like Iranians, and access to formal citizenship has not changed the racial structure of German society and the longer history of ancestry-based citizenship and national identity. A foreigner has more legal protections with a passport, but race-based conceptions of social membership persist, which is why foreigners are discriminated against despite being German citizens. When I asked Kasra about citizenship and equality, he distinguished between the law and ordinary Germans:

It's just a piece of paper. You will never be a German. I have never known myself to be a German; it's just a piece of paper. And the other person, if they were to ask you where you are from and you answer, "German," they'd say, "Well, you're a *Schwarzkopf*. You have dark eyes," and they'd say, "You have a German passport, but you're not German."

Kasra elaborates on Paul's point of "to that person I'm a foreigner" by talking about the idea of "authentically German." Iranians can become naturalized citizens and access the privileges that come with citizenship, but you will be reminded, "you're not German, you are a *Schwarzkopf*." Formal citizenship provides legal protections and rights, but does not mean that one becomes German, it does not change how you look, or the importance of ancestry and race in Germany—"it is only a piece of paper."[17] Citizenship also does not guarantee that one will be treated equally; you can possess a German passport and still suffer from discrimination and marginality. Anna, a second-generation Iranian woman born and raised in Hamburg, was finishing her vocational program in fashion design at the time of our interview. When I asked her similar questions about citizenship, she told me:

It's very hard here to see oneself as being from here, they even say it, they say you are "plastic Deutsch." That means that what it says on your passport is plastic, you are a plastic Deutsch . . . there is a difference between being a foreigner, becoming a naturalized citizen, and being a German from the beginning. For example, my cousin—she was born here and automatically got a German passport. She never had an Iranian one, and she is still the same as me, she still has black hair.

This sort of reference to being "a German on paper" versus phenotypically looking like one is a frequent one. Anna's reference to "being a German from the beginning" implies this ancestry-based idea of German identity. Being born in Germany or becoming a naturalized citizen does not erase the importance and centrality of racial/ethnic and cultural background and phenotypic features. Racial categories and distinctions continue to carry weight and influence throughout German society, which means that those who have foreign ancestry are marginalized. Access to formal citizenship cannot disrupt the ways in which race and ancestry function and are used throughout German civil society and institutions. Possessing a German passport places Iranians in the category of "naturalized citizen," but they remain "plastic Deutsch."

The experiences of the interlocutors demonstrate how race and culture are meaningful and significant boundaries between Germans and foreigners. The interviews illustrate that Iranians experience Germany to be a racial state. Kasra's charge that "in Germany, no matter what you do, you will always be a foreigner" is substantiated by the stories of many Iranians in Germany. Lived experience had confirmed that formal citizenship would neither make them German nor guarantee them equal opportunity and treatment. Realistically only those of German descent are afforded that. Having German citizenship has not made Iranians feel like they are equal to Germans. Rather, being an *Ausländer* and treated like a *Schwarzkopf* is a considerable barrier to Iranians experiencing unqualified acceptance, belonging, and equality. They lack social membership. Moreover, they experience Germany to be a place that has preserved a conception of German identity rooted in race (ancestry), which means that those with the "right ancestry" can attain unconditional belonging. Iranians' experiences align with Germany's longer history of "the Herrenvolk" and theories of race and Aryanism. A Herrenvolk democracy, as described by Mills (1997), is a "white republic" that is founded upon the "notion of racial, Anglo-Saxonist 'manifest destiny'" (p. 40). The notion that ancestry makes someone "echt Deutsch" (real German) is still very present in twenty-first-century Germany, and the Herrenvolk[18] ideologies, which earlier determined white rights and freedoms and made sure they were protected, are still present and show up, although in different ways and degrees, in current-day Germany.

Limitations to Mobility

While many Iranians believed that race and ancestry still mattered in Germany, there were differences in opinion about whether social and cultural integration would manifest into better and equal treatment and opportunities for upward mobility. Yes, Iranians were able to utilize and benefit from Germany's social-insurance programs and economically and politically participate in German society, but economic mobility and professional advancement were more difficult to access. While these barriers were most common among the first-generation migrants, second-generation[19] Iranian migrants also complained of persistent anti-foreigner prejudice and discrimination: in school they were placed in tracks that made it difficult to enter the gymnasium track, they faced challenges entering desired vocational programs, and they were persistently placed in ill-suited work by the state employment bureau and experienced sustained periods of unemployment.

Barriers to Advancement

Siavash was a first-generation Iranian who had lived in Germany for seven years and had been an electrical technician prior to his migration. He explained that despite having been approved for a vocational program (*Ausbildung*) to be a certified electrician, the German employment bureau had refused to pay for it. When I asked why, he replied:

> Because I was a foreigner—there was no other reason why I should not have been approved. I am sure that if I were a German, I would have gotten them to approve the training. I wanted to get a lawyer but heard that it would make the situation even worse, maybe even jeopardize my safety. I know that if this had been approved, the next ten years of my life would have been set. I would be set here in Germany.

Experiences like Siavash's were not rare; many Iranians shared stories of unfair treatment at the Arbeitsamt, the employment bureau, in their pursuit of work and vocational training opportunities. For many, the employment office was a key site of discrimination; it was accused of systematically placing foreigners into low-skilled work, even when job candidates were clearly qualified for higher positions. Siavash was certain that if he had been German, they would have approved and paid for the program, as they "ultimately prefer a German to have the better-paying jobs that come with more extensive pensions." Siavash also felt that filing a complaint against the employment bureau could produce more problems for him, possibly impacting his pending asylum case.[20] Despite having been accepted into an electrician-apprenticeship program, he was fearful of having his asylum case rejected, which ultimately led him to accept a job as a warehouse worker.

Similarly, second-generation Iranians also felt that Germans failed to treat them equally, even though by all accounts, they were deeply integrated. They felt that their foreign ancestry affected them at school, the gymnasium especially, vocational training opportunities, and professional advancement. When I asked Kasra whether racial/ethnic background mattered in Germany, he replied:

Yes, it has affected my chance to get a job, because the guy sitting at the desk and reading my résumé—this is how I think, I don't know if I'm wrong, I could be wrong—but the minute they read the name and see the picture, they say, "Oh, that's how he thinks." I've been here for twenty-five years, and that's my sense of things. They see me and say, "Okay, so he's done this and done that." But not until my work is ten times better than someone else, I won't get the job. . . . I went to this place and tried to apply for a job, and they said that my hair was not blond and that they didn't want me. I laughed. I was not even upset, because my friend worked there and said they are crazy. When they looked at my résumé, they knew I did good work, but said that I did not fit their group. They did not say this to me directly but told my friend.

When a foreigner applies for a job—regardless of their education, skills, and work experience—they will encounter management that will likely employ stereotypical thinking, make negative assumptions about foreigners, and ultimately discriminate against those with non-German ancestry. Kasra feels that the added requirement to include a picture in German job applications, in essence, allows employers to use phenotypic features as criteria for hiring. In other words, practices of racial/ethnic profiling assess the employability of candidates by how "foreign looking" they appear, which inevitably disadvantages the job prospects of those with darker phenotypic features, those who "look foreign," and women who are veiled.[21] What is more, unless a foreigner is professionally overqualified or perceived as being different from the average "stereotypical foreigner," they will be ascribed a set of negative stereotypes.

This drawback of having foreign ancestry was also pronounced for Anahita, a second-generation respondent who had lived in Germany since the age of five and had German citizenship, a degree in international finance, and fluency in five languages. Before she found work in the field of international finance, she discussed how her identity as an Iranian and a woman had produced challenges in the labor market after graduating from the university. She said this about how foreign ancestry affects employment opportunities:

> Why can't I get the job when I'm the most qualified? After I graduated from the Uni I was unemployed for three months. I remember going to see this woman at the employee office and she told me that she didn't want to believe how well my grades were. And when she checked all my work, she said that if it were between a German and me, the German would get the job. She said that if she were a manager or boss at a company, she'd also choose a German over me. I told her that's precisely why I was forced to be at the unemployment bureau and live off 400 euros a month.

Anahita felt that she had done everything correctly; she had lived in Germany her whole life, spoke fluent German, was a German citizen, socialized with mostly Germans, had changed her name for job applications, did not look "visibly foreign," and graduated from university in international finance with top grades. Theoretically, all of this should have afforded her plenty of employment opportunities. However, time and time again, experiences in the labor market illustrated that ancestry still mattered and that German candidates were preferred over her. Although she was often overqualified, she felt that she had missed out on important employment opportunities because of her ancestry. She changed her name so that—at least on paper—the disadvantage of her foreign ancestry in the labor market might be ameliorated. A name change, a coping strategy and response to racial discrimination and blocked mobility in the job market, was mentioned by several respondents. Although most agreed that it was a short-term measure, and as Anahita argued, "I'm not this person. I can't just become Mueller overnight," changing "foreign-sounding" names is seemingly common practice among Iranians.

While Iranians may be "well-integrated foreigners," they still encounter a very real social boundary that limits their employment and professional opportunities.[22] These experiences demonstrate that length of residence, holding a German passport, or being educated in Germany do not mean that one is no longer a foreigner; the mark of being foreign is experienced as something that is enduring and perpetual. Iranians can utilize some of the opportunities available in Germany with an understanding that they must become as close to the majority group as possible while still not being able to attain same opportunities as Germans. Pari had worked in various German institutions the past thirty-plus years. Although she considered herself well integrated—she was college educated, a fluent German speaker, with two grown children who were of mixed German and Iranian background—she detailed experiences of marginality and discrimination. She told me:

> For myself, it was about being a foreigner and being Iranian. I've had many experiences like that. In 1993, I was working at the ministry and

had applied for a job promotion, a higher position. And the boss told me that unfortunately we have chosen someone else. I told him that I was after a better job, because my salary, compared to others in my position, was the lowest. He said that I was self-confident, that this is a good thing, but realistically when he was in the US and lived there for a few years, he never allowed himself as a foreigner in the US to apply for a higher position. And you hear this from the boss of your department. . . . I leaned right into him and told him, "You know I had come to Germany in 1973, I have been here for twenty years, and I have paid taxes for twenty years, my children live here, and my children will continue to live here, and so will my grandchildren. I allow myself to even apply to work at the state department." He understood that what he had said was bad and he quickly tried to cover up his statement, became apologetic. This racism is somewhat hidden but is plentiful here.

Discrimination and racism is commonplace in Germany, especially in the labor market, and non-Germans can only excel and climb to certain levels; all doors and avenues are not open to non-Germans. Pari has been passed up for promotions and greater job opportunities because she is not German. She also told me that length of residency or educational attainment does not translate into being able to equally access resources. She mentioned how having a German spouse can make life in Germany easier in some ways—and many Iranians who had married Germans spoke of the things it does provide—but it cannot alter or lessen the "foreign aspects" of her identity. There is also a sentiment that is hidden in the conversation with her past manager—that Germans "were kind enough to accept foreigners into their country, but now they are asking for too much." The sense that "foreigners should know their place" is something that Pari felt that Germans typically aim to convey to foreigners, and her old manager did this by recounting his work experiences in the US and how he did not have the gall to expect Americans to promote him to a higher position or treat him equally.

The stories of the Iranian interlocutors emphasize the continued importance of race/ethnic background in German institutions. All the interlocutors possessed permanent legal residency and the majority had a German passport. If we were to use conventional markers and measures of integration,[23] then there is no doubt that the Iranians that participated in this research are all well integrated into German society. However, in all the cases presented, Iranians believed that it was their ancestry—not qualifications or lack of integration—that kept them from attaining better opportunities. It is having foreign ancestry and being Muslim—or perceived as Muslim—that racialize, stigmatize, and limit opportunities for Iranians and other migrant populations. Iranians believed that being a foreigner was a racially marked identity, and that it was perpetual, not something that would disappear within a few generations. Ultimately, the refusal of Germans to fully accept foreigners of different racial backgrounds remains a contentious and painful issue; as will be seen, this resurfaces significantly after the 2015 refugee crisis.

The 2015 Refugee Crisis

The 2015 refugee crisis created a humanitarian crisis in Europe of a kind unseen since World War II. Approximately four million Syrians have been displaced since 2011, most of them living in refugee camps in Turkey, Lebanon, and Pakistan.[24] A number of factors have facilitated this, including the political uprisings during the summer of 2011, the ongoing civil war in Syria, the war in Iraq, and rising inequality and poverty across a number of Middle Eastern and African countries, specifically Syria, Iraq, Afghanistan, Sudan, and Somalia.[25] Of the four million Syrian refugees displaced outside of Syria, approximately 1.3 million arrived in Europe in September 2015. While the refugee crisis is considered to be the "largest migration crisis" in Europe since World War II,[26] not all EU member states were willing to accept refugees. Italy, Greece, and the UK—in particular—had large-scale anti-refugee protests in support of keeping refugees out. Nationalism and Islamophobia were the underlying forces that helped create massive opposition toward the acceptance of refugees. Germany was the only exception. Angela Merkel, Germany's chancellor, declared in September 2015 that refugees were welcome in Germany. It is estimated that in 2015 Germany took in approximately 800,000 refugees from Syria, Afghanistan, and Iraq; some officials place the estimate at 1.2 million.[27] Given Germany's history of racial nationalism and anti-foreigner prejudice, I returned to Hamburg in the summer of 2016 wondering how the acceptance of 1.2 million refugees impacted existing arrangements and boundaries between native and immigrant populations. Had Iranians' experiences shifted or changed since I was there in 2011? Had the rise of right-wing political groups intensified the racialization of foreigners, especially Muslims?

The 2016 interviews and fieldwork elaborate on how critical international events, like the 2015 refugee crisis, affect the "immigrant-native" boundary, processes of racialization, and existing racial/ethnic hierarchies. Similar to the US and nations like France, the Netherlands, Italy, Greece, etc., Germany is also experiencing a revival and reemergence of right-wing political groups and movements centered on anti-immigrant, anti-refugee, and anti-Muslim rhetoric and policy. A clear example of this is the rise and popularity of the AfD.[28] A political party rooted in "traditional Christian Values" and anti-immigrant and anti-refugee ideology and policy, the AfD was able to secure 12 percent of the German parliament in 2017, something unseen since the days of Nazism. In October 2019, the AfD took nearly 24 percent, one percentage point higher than Angela Merkel's party, the Christian Democrats (CDU).[29] Similar to the US, the changing climate has brought to light buried sentiments and prejudices that Iranians had assumed had somewhat subsided.[30] Many were shocked that, after thirty or forty years of living in Germany, they were seen as foreigners again, treated as outsiders, and even publicly insulted and harassed. Changed interactions with Germans had made Iranians anxious about the future of Germany, their place in it, and whether they would "always be foreigners" in Germany.

Rise of Racial Nationalism

A central narrative that I encountered upon returning to Hamburg was that Germans were acting cautious and standoffish; some were even "saying things they had not in years." This entailed expressing prejudice toward foreigners and making explicit comments that lumped all foreigners—established immigrant communities and the newly arriving refugees—together. Iranians seemed especially upset that Germans whom they had known for years, such as their neighbors, coworkers, and local butchers and bakers, were not willing to distinguish between them and the new refugees. In her 2011 interview, Buye Gandom had a positive assessment of Germany, her professional opportunities as an engineer, and the treatment of foreigners in Germany. In the 2016 follow up interview, she discussed some changes:

> A few years ago, it didn't seem like Germans had this very particular view toward foreigners, they didn't have all these preconceived notions of foreigners or refugees. . . . Now, we have groups like the AfD that say a bunch of crap. Like this woman was saying that "now that Germany has been eliminated from the Euro-Cup, we need to go forward with an all-German team," although half of the German team has foreign roots. Two years ago, you would not hear such statements; they wouldn't allow themselves to say such things, because of the things they did in the past. Even if someone thought this way, they wouldn't express it. Now, because of the waves of refugees that came in 2015, they do.

Buye Gandom described how public and political discourse about foreigners had shifted in the past two years. German nationalism and anti-foreigner prejudice were on the rise, and Germans were increasingly crossing certain boundaries. She felt that in previous years Germans would have been reluctant to call for an "all German" soccer team or support the rise of political groups like the AfD. She also points out how German nationalism continues to be associated with Nazism and makes an indirect reference to the Holocaust by commenting that Germans used to be more cautious because of the "things they did in the past." David, a second-generation professional, echoed the shifts described by Buye Gandom. He said this about changes in public discourse since the refugee crisis:

> Among some Germans, their treatment and interactions have changed. Before it was somewhere in the middle, and now it's become extreme; some support a lot and some do not. Its extreme polarization, like the Trump and Sanders camp in the US. And a lot of anti-foreigner rhetoric has become acceptable again. It's acceptable to say again, "If these foreigners want to demonstrate and are dissatisfied, then they can return to their own countries." Before, this was a very racist thing to say, because a foreigner who has a German passport has a right to protest, to exercise their rights. So negative discourse against foreigners seems to have become more acceptable.

David points toward the rise of right-leaning populism and the dangers of a polarizing political environment by comparing what was happening in Germany to the 2016 US presidential election. He felt that the rise of right-leaning populist parties and anti-immigrant rhetoric had given ordinary Germans permission to be "openly racist." Foreigners who voiced their opinions or dissatisfaction about social or political matters were increasingly met with a discourse of "go back to your country." This very deeply impacts Iranians' ability to feel and see themselves as equal, as having social citizenship, and as participants in national matters and conversations. Again, we see foreigners being told that "they should know their place" and that they should be grateful to have been received in Germany and provided a place for permanent residency. But they should not mistakenly think that they are equal to Germans or have the right to reciprocal participation. Formal German citizenship while providing legal protections does not create a sense of social membership. David continued to comment on how the changing social and political climate was affecting day-to-day interactions:

> Many Germans portrayed themselves as very open minded, but then something happens in the media, like this sexual assault incident during New Year's Eve 2015. . . . In the last fifteen years, I have not been the subject of racial slurs. But recently, I was promoting my business, and someone walked by and made an anti-foreigner slur. And given my profession, I have built thick skin, so it does not bother me as much anymore, but one can sense that they are looking at you with different eyes, a different glance. We were on the path of being accepted; then they use phrases like "you foreigners" or "all foreigners," and everyone is lumped together again.

As detailed in the following section, Iranians considered the incidents of New Year's Eve 2015 as pivotal in changing how Germans viewed those with foreign ancestry—specifically, that Germans now had "a reason to express the anti-foreigner racism that they long harbored." David points out that the likelihood of having tense and hostile public encounters, like the one he experienced, had risen because of the "more racist" environment. Public racism was seemingly acceptable again, and Iranians were increasingly experiencing ordinary Germans partaking in vigilante behavior and the policing of public space.

New Year's Eve 2015

New Year's Eve 2015 (Sylvester Night) was repeatedly cited as a critical event that changed the public narrative around and people's opinions of refugees, Muslims, and those with Middle Eastern ancestry. It greatly heightened anxiety and fear among Iranians, as if they were bracing themselves for what was to come. Buye Gandom had this to say:

> There was the incident in Cologne during the New Year 2015 where foreign men were groping and sexually molesting and assaulting women. So

when this happened you see that Germans have become more standoff-ish. Even the people who used to be more open-minded are starting to become standoffish and take a step back.

The media reported that groups of primarily foreign men sexually harassed and assaulted young women, especially German women. This created a major outcry around the nation; many claimed that the "newly accepted refugees" behaved in this manner because of their culture and Islam.[31] These stories, which were widely reported in the German press and social media, were "believable" because they relied upon long-standing tropes rooted in colonialism and Orientalism. Cainkar's (2009) analysis of the racism and Islamophobia that Arab Americans and Muslims experienced after 9/11 is useful here. She argued that this racism did not begin with 9/11, but rather that it "was rooted in preexist-ing ideas and social constructions that configured them as people who would readily conduct and approve of such attacks" (p. 2). The case of Cologne on New Year's Eve is similar in that the rise of anti-foreigner racism in the media and the rise in negative treatment that Iranians and other foreigners experienced after that day is not solely about Cologne, about a single event. It was about a much larger history of the vilification of Muslim, Middle Eastern, and North African migrant populations. Buye Gandom recalled that even Germans who were more liberal and progressive in their thinking had begun to pull back and become some standoffish. She went on to describe how the media coverage and dis-cussions surrounding this event played out on social media:

There was security footage from the disco and women were crying and saying that "they were Arabian and trying to rape us." This was a big scan-dal. After Sylvester everything changed, and people started writing on social media and Facebook that "enough is enough. We took you into our homeland, we helped you and this is your response to our helping hand. It's not our problem that your religion will not allow you to have relation-ships with women."

The discourse that these newly admitted foreigners were taking advantage of German hospitality and humanitarianism became a central theme in the press and social media.[32] This was significantly gendered and centered on men. Weber (2016) illustrates how German press and populist political groups were swiftly circulating narratives of male refugees as inherent sexual predators after the events of Cologne. The narrative of "uncivilized" Arab and Muslim men with repressed sexual identities coming from Syria, Afghanistan, and Iraq who were not accustomed to the values, norms, and practices of Western society and unable to control themselves from ogling at women and harassing them in public became a central storyline in the news and social media. Additionally, some in the media associated these attacks with Islam, depicting Muslims and non-Western culture as antithetical to Western democratic standards and practices. It was believed that this event further racialized Middle Eastern foreigners, including Iranians, because of the stereotype that all foreign men were traditional, misogynistic, disrespectful, and inherently anti-Western. Isabel also saw Sylvester Night 2015 as a turning point, an event that changed public and political commentary about foreigners. She explained how it impacted her relationships and encounters with Germans in public spaces:

> After Sylvester, everything in Germany changed, really everything. . . . This was the first time I would go out on the streets and I felt like, "Holy shit, they're all looking at me." This was the first time. And I was like, "Okay, maybe, if the time passes on it will be different." But no . . . you know, I was a person full of self-esteem and self-confidence. Everywhere I went, I was accepted. Now I come in and say hello, and nobody's responding and you're like "shit" . . . like if you want to go to the mall. In the mall, everywhere you go it was, "Hi, how are you, can I help you?" But now it's not like that. Now you go in a restaurant or something, and you're sitting there and sitting there and you're waiting, you're waiting, and waiting.

Like what I heard in 2011, foreign men seemed to bear the brunt of anti-Muslim and anti-foreigner racism more intensely, but recently even women were mistreated. These changes had a profound impact on Isabel's self-confidence and self-esteem; she felt increasingly fearful in public spaces. In all the thirty-plus years that Isabel had lived in Germany, she had never experienced this sense of alienation and exclusion from German society, had not experienced differential treatment at the mall, grocery store, restaurant. She was one of the respondents who had only positive accounts of German society in her 2011 interview and was one of the interlocutors who had experienced gross changes when we spoke five years later. It is notable that while the event took place in Cologne—a city four hours south of Hamburg—immigrant groups in Hamburg and across Germany felt stigmatized and noticed the chilling effect that this had on their social relationships and encounters with Germans in the days and weeks to follow. As illustrated through the changing discourse about refugees and their culture, Islam is increasingly articulated as a collection of "lacks" and Muslims as "premodern," the "antithesis" to German society, and that the acceptance of refugees has "become our nightmare." Sylvester Night further perpetuated the idea of foreigners as irreconcilable with German secularity, humanism, and liberty.

Fear and Vigilantism

My conversations with Iranians illustrate more fear and increased experience with marginality since the refugee crisis. Daily activities like going to work, taking public transportation, and shopping at the grocery store had all become sites of potential exclusion and difference. Some felt especially stigmatized and threatened in public spaces and their place of business; this was particularly acute for small-business owners and professionals. The social climate had shifted boundaries, and relationships between Germans and immigrant communities were changing for the worse. Isabel shared an incident in which she became a target of a racist and sexist verbal attack on the train:

One day I was coming from work, and I was sitting in the metro and the metro was full of people. There was a drunken person on the train—he was dressed very good—he looked at me and started cursing and calling me a "pussy" and "slut." At first, I was shocked: "Like, is he talking to me?" And then he proceeded to yell at me that I was a "foreigner slut, and that we have to kill all of you and bury you." I'm not the kind of person to not respond, but I was so shocked, I was like frozen, I couldn't respond.

This kind of racist and violent behavior on the part of ordinary Germans was becoming more common throughout Germany. This incident came as a total shock to Isabel. In her 2011 interview, she expressed a sense of belonging and saw herself as an equal member of German society—she had struggled to think of a situation in which she was ever treated differently than a German. But since the refugee crisis, there had been several encounters, some minor and a few more extreme, that had cast doubt about whether she still belonged there. This incident had shaken her, and she changed several of her behaviors and routines as a result. For example, she told me that she got her driver's license and started driving to avoid getting on public transportation. When I inquired about whether she had heard of others who had encounters on the train, she immediately replied:

Yes, a similar thing happened to my husband. He was coming from work, and he was dressed well. And there was a seat facing a German woman and he took the seat. She said "okay," then stood up and switched her seat. He is dressed well, he does not look like a refugee; you can see that, he even has a ring on his ring finger. This hurt me much more than my own experience. My husband would not do anything to anyone, and it makes me more upset when something happens to him. He does not deserve it. And that has changed, and it would be much easier to just say "these assholes, German Nazis," but the bad thing is I can understand their feelings and their changing behavior.

Isabel believed that Germans had changed their behavior toward foreigners because they felt that "all foreigners were the same," the same as the people behind the Cologne event. The racial boundaries between immigrants and natives—or German and foreigners—seemed to have become bright and rigid, once again. But interestingly, Isabel did not blame Germans for their racism. Rather, she agreed that newly arriving refugees were to blame because they were taking advantage of the German system and that Germans had a right to feel uncomfortable. So, while she increasingly felt like a second-class citizen and had in recent months changed her name to bypass employment discrimination, had become a German citizen, and gotten her driver's license after this incident to avoid public transportation, she still thought that Germans were justified in acting differently. Implicit in Isabel's commentary is that "new foreigners" are not behaving like good, integrated ones and thus are making life harder for all foreigners. If refugees integrated more quickly, if they learned to "act right" then Germans would not react in prejudiced ways. Isabel did not name nationalism or the lingering racism in German society as facilitating the rise of vigilantism but doubled down on integrationist discourse and essentially placed the blame for the increased racism in Germany on the actions and behaviors of the newly arriving refugees. This is a common response to racism by Iranians who have been racialized and marginalized, and I analyze this dissonance in more detail in the next chapter.

Kimia, who had lived in Germany since the late 1970s, also spoke of changed interactions with Germans. She began by recounting how Iranians, like herself, had been hesitant to publicly speak Persian in the past, even advising family visiting from Iran to not express an "Iranian temperament" in front of Germans. She commented that "this fear was a long time ago, but the feeling is back." She then described a recent encounter with a neighbor whom she had known for many years:

> I said hello, like normal; he quickly said hi and walked by fast, so I ran after him. He pulled himself back, like don't touch me. I said, "What's

REFUGEES AND AUSLÄNDERS | 115

going on, I haven't been around for a while, I was gone, I am happy to see you." He said that "we can interact to this extent, but not more." When I asked why, what had happened, he proceeded to yell very loudly, saying, "All these foreigners have been accepted, Merkel this and that, she needs to be fired," just ranting about several things. And then I said, "Hey, it's me you're talking to, what is going on with you?" And he responded, "These people are everywhere, standing around, I am scared everywhere I go."

After forty-five minutes of calmly speaking with her neighbor, her neighbor finally admitted that "he didn't mean 'her or her family' when he expressed anti-foreigner" prejudice. This exchange had brought back negative memories of being mistreated in public, the fear of being a foreigner, and feelings of not belonging in Germany. For example, it took her back to a time when her local butcher, whose shop she frequently patronized, had said "these foreigners" in conversation with another customer in front of her. After she confronted him, he responded with "I did not mean you or your family." So when Kimia's neighbor—someone she had known for two decades—had felt comfortable making offensive statements about foreigners, it evoked buried feelings of exclusion. This incident was yet another reminder of what she explained in her 2011 interview when she commented that "they are not obliged to accept me, and I think many Iranians forget. Germans have no obligations or responsibilities for us. We have no inheritance or part of this place; we can try to integrate ourselves if we want to."

Changed relationships with German coworkers, neighbors, and acquaintances were more common in the 2016 interviews. As Buye Gandom, David, Isabel, Kimia, and Pari all remarked, Germans had become more cautious and colder, and were openly making disparaging statements about foreigners. There was a rise of prejudice and racism in interpersonal and public settings and Iranians were experiencing it first-hand. David reflected upon the kind of prejudice and discrimination that he believed would increase:

The informal discrimination is more, and its mostly implicit and it's hard to prove. When looking for places to live, trying to get work, the day to day, the daily tasks, and encounters. It's the way they speak with you, talk with you, their body language.

David described the more implicit, implied, and nuanced ways in which foreigners, including Iranians, would be marginalized or made to feel uncomfortable and unwanted. Like Isabel—who spoke of being looked at differently, as if she did not belong in Germany—David also gave an account that evidenced the subtleness of the prejudice Iranians were now experiencing: the way you are spoken to by Germans, they language they use, and their body language. Iranians throughout the follow-up interviews were acutely aware of the changes that were taking place. David's assertion that this kind of racism is often difficult to prove because of its more implicit and personal nature is evident in the work of Selod (2015), who calls attention to the "role of private citizens" in stripping Muslim Americans of aspects of social citizenship. In both the US and Germany, it was private white citizens who had engaged in vigilante behaviors, including watching Iranians with suspicion and verbally assaulting and publicly harassing them. The follow-up interviews vividly show how the intensification of interpersonal prejudice and racial micro-aggressions has made interactions with Germans more strained and increased the odds of negative face-to-face encounters. Changes to the social and political climate, in this case driven by a refugee crisis, brighten existing boundaries and intensify the construction of social marginality. This is especially the case in nations with a legacy of ancestry-based distinctions and racial nationalism where race is seldom erased from all components of national culture, thinking, and structures in a society. In these contexts, racism, racial nationalism, and processes of racialization intensify and wane in relation to social and political climate and culture. The follow-up interviews in both nations highlighted these shifts.

Discussion

Germany has made significant strides toward becoming a socially democratic, humanitarian, refugee-accepting society, yet deep-rooted racial nationalism remains. Throughout this chapter, first- and second-generation Iranians have described the unique challenges presented by living in a nation that accepts refugees and asylum seekers yet maintains ethnic nationalism and anti-foreigner tendencies. The interviews reveal the varying sentiments and experiences of Iranians in Germany.

In Germany, the attainment of middle-class and upper-middle-class status is the exception, not the norm. Those who came before the 1979 revolution were educated in Germany, were actively sought by German companies and universities during the Pahlavi era (these Iranians occupy very specific and specialized jobs), and were more likely to succeed financially. There were also a few Iranians who had become successful business owners. However, there were also plenty of educated Iranians who faced a limited labor market, worked ill-suited jobs, and relied on social welfare. Being on social welfare was not necessarily an indicator for having low human capital or a lack of formal education, but rather a consequence of labor market discrimination. While second-generation Iranians differed in important ways than the first—by speaking German fluently, being more well-versed in German cultural norms and practices, and having gone through the German education system—they still faced structural barriers. They spoke of teacher bias and educational tracking, with teachers recommending some students (mostly German) to the gymnasium track, leading them to go to the university, but leaving students of foreign background out. They also spoke of an explicit preference for German employees. These limitations and barriers in the German educational system and labor market are widely cited by European scholars, highlighting how the attainment of credentials and skills is still not equally available to non-Germans despite their immigration and citizenship background, length of residence, and other conventional measures of integration.[33]

The idea of being "perpetually foreign" was also a consistent theme throughout the German interviews. Iranians feel that they can take advantage of some opportunities with an understanding that they are guests in Germany. If a foreigner learns the German language, abides by established laws and customs, and adopts and integrates German cultural norms and practices, they are understood to be a "well-integrated foreigner." Symbolic boundaries can be crossed by partaking in social events and holidays, fraternizing and developing friendships with Germans, and becoming involved in German organizations and institutions, However, the reality of the social boundary is there, which means that opportunity structures related to higher-level professional occupations and promotions are mostly closed off to non-Germans. Foreigners, including Iranians, are aware that, though they can approximate belonging and social membership, they will never be "real Germans." Despite having lived in Germany for decades or being born there, they are unable to access social citizenship and an unconditional feeling of belonging because social membership in Germany is still tied to having German ancestry. The experiences of the Iranians I spoke with fall in line with the larger history of German racial nationalism, race/ancestry-based conceptions of German identity, and German nation-state making.

In the latter part of the chapter, I also demonstrated how the refugee crisis has heightened the racialization of refugees from Muslim-majority nations and reawakened feelings of perpetual foreignness among Iranians. The 2016 interviews revealed great anxiety, fear, and feelings of uncertainty among Iranians in ways that were not evident in 2010–2011. The acceptance of refugees since 2015 has aroused the dormant and deep-rooted anxieties, prejudice, and racism that Germans had toward foreigners and Muslims. The rise of the AfD and increasing anti-migrant and anti-Muslim movements are some examples of this. Their rise illustrates that German racial nationalism was never eliminated, but had been simmering below the surface. Far-right movements in Germany and throughout Europe have made foreigners even more hypervisible, increasing their sense of being perpetual foreigners. Consequently, Iranians and other non-German populations question whether Germany is as accepting of foreigners as it formerly was and whether they will ever be seen and treated as legitimate members of German society.

The reemergence of feeling like "foreigners all over again" is tied to the changing social and political climate in Germany. Iranians have found themselves feeling increasingly anxious and uncomfortable about their future in Germany, something they did not express in the prior interviews. These perceptions and experiences of we "will never be real Germans" fall in line with the larger history of racial nationalism, nation-state making, and lack of immigration policy. Iranians understand that foreigners have no birthright in Germany—that this is not their homeland, and they are "guests." That Germany has been "kind enough" to accept them is something I heard on numerous occasions.

The next chapter will delve deeper into how processes of stigmatization and racialization are detrimental to belonging and how they produce experiences of "conditional belonging," perpetual foreignness, and outsider status for Iranians in both the US and Germany. I will also provide a more thorough analysis of how Iranians have responded to and coped with the racialization and politicization that they have experienced the past forty years. These reactions vary based on national context. One that is seen explicitly in the 2016 follow-up interviews is an emerging disdain toward the newly received refugees among some Iranians in Germany. Not surprisingly, some are swift to create distance between themselves and those "bad foreigners" who threaten the position and status of Iranians. I consider the "good foreigners" ideal—a variation of the model minority trope—as a response to their racialization and marginalization and anxieties about their place in Germany. These dynamics will become evident when I examine the type of efforts Iranians employ to explicitly prove (*beweisen*) to Germans that Iranians have similar interests and lifestyles as them and that they know how to "act and behave properly."

4

Racial and Cultural Flexibility

Conditional Belonging in the United States and Germany

In the last two chapters, I teased apart experiences that were more specific to the policies and climate of the US and Germany, including geopolitics, asylum and immigration policy, and the existing racial ideologies and racialized social structures. In chapter 2, I demonstrated that being persistently associated with the actions and policies of the Iranian government has resulted in the Iranian community being racialized and politically stigmatized. Very rarely do we see a distinction made between Iranians and the Iranian government; they are overwhelmingly seen as being one and the same. The demonization of Iran and thus Iranian immigrants became even more intense with Donald Trump's election as president. The possibility of attaining long-term diplomatic relations through the Iran Deal ended, and the follow-up interviews reflect these shifts and emphasize deep concerns among Iranians. They worry about the continued economic sanctions against Iran, the Muslim Ban, and the possibility of military conflict. The current social and political climate has also made Iranians question the narrative of the US being a "nation of immigrants" and their ability to live in comfort and safety. Compared to the Obama era, racism feels more intense and explicitly targets immigrants and non-white communities. The rise in white nativism and right-wing politics has cast some doubt on whether Iranians will be able to truly feel like they belong in the US. It is still uncertain whether this trend will change in the Biden era.

In chapter 3, I illustrated that the political relationship between Iran and Germany is not hostile; there are no military threats, no naval standoffs in the Persian Gulf, and no travel restrictions against those of

Iranian ancestry. Diplomatic relations between the nations have continued since the 1979 Iranian Revolution as seen by the presence of Iranian consulates in the cities of Hamburg, Frankfurt, and Munich, and an embassy in Berlin. Travel between the two countries is relatively easy, and direct flights between Tehran and major German cities take place multiple times a week. Iranians are also not surveilled in Germany and, for the most part, not considered to be "foreign enemies" to Germany or Germans. The marginality that Iranians confront is mostly rooted in German racial nationalism and anti-foreigner racism rather than German-Iranian political relations. Being categorized and seen as an *Ausländer*, as a *Schwarzkopf*, as someone who has no "real inheritance" or roots in Germany is cited by many as the cause of much of the racism and discrimination they have experienced. It was very rare that Germans said something negative about Iranians specifically. Many of the latter lamented that Germany's acceptance of 1.2 million new refugees in 2015 had made Germans more suspicious of foreigners, making them feel like "we will always be foreigners." Vigilante behavior, racial slurs, and verbal assaults by private citizens, ordinary Germans, had taken Iranians by surprise. This rise of overt racism and anti-foreigner prejudice had also heightened the sense of "being watched" and "being profiled." Anxiety over the rise and growth of right-wing movements was vivid in the 2016 follow-up interviews and provided a bright illustration of how changes to the sociopolitical climate can and do impact experiences of belonging and social membership.

This chapter has several objectives. First, it aims to examine the most common coping mechanisms Iranians have developed in response to being racialized and marginalized. Second, it aims to provide a deeper examination of how the existing racial stratification systems in the US and Germany provide the conditions for "racial flexibility" in the US and "cultural flexibility" in Germany. I define racial flexibility "as the ability to bend and shift, and shape how one is racially/ethnically perceived through several conscious and deliberate decisions," whereas cultural flexibility "involves a set of gestures meant to signal and express cultural proximity to Germans." And third, it highlights the consequences and implications that being racially othered has on belonging and social membership. The chapter also considers why social citizenship and belonging are susceptible to, and always in conversation with, national and global social and political climate. Lastly, it makes the case that persistent racialization and politicization have created a sense of "conditional belonging" for Iranian migrants and the feeling that "unconditional belonging" and equal access to social citizenship and membership is not available for them. The chapter concludes with a discussion of why integrationist frameworks or casting some immigrants as "model minorities" or "quintessential foreigners" will not erase the role that race and culture play in nations that maintain racialized social structures.[1]

Managing Racialization

Experiences of racial discrimination and marginality have had a profound impact on the lives of Iranians in the diaspora, and avoiding further discrimination and racism often leads Iranian immigrants to develop coping mechanisms to alleviate, ameliorate, or escape marginality. That is, it is common to attempt to *manage* racialization by hiding and downplaying racial/ethnic and religious identity, embracing racial ambiguity, attempting to pass or be seen as another racial/ethnic group, hiding one's ethnic background or ancestry, not speaking Persian in public, anglicizing names, changing one's phenotypic appearance,[2] and endeavoring to "prove" that one is "a good foreigner." I consider each to be a form of coping, "a way to work around" racism and marginality. They should also be read as efforts at belonging and social membership in nations where historically "unconditional belonging" has been available only to those of the dominant white racial group. The similarities and differences in coping strategies in the US and Germany, I suggest, significantly relate to the dominant racial and cultural ideologies and boundaries that operate in each nation.

Racial Ambiguity and Racial Flexibility

Iranians are not necessarily wrong in their thinking that they might be able to "melt" into the melting pot, especially given their official racial status as white[3] in the US. Being officially classified as white gives them this sense that they are closer to whiteness than those categorized as non-white, a taste of "symbolic whiteness."[4] This whiteness, though, is liminal, and Iranians and other South West Asian and North African (SWANA) populations do not necessarily reap the social benefits of it.[5]

The limitations of white racial classification for Iranians are seen in the strides they make to conceal their identity, or even pass as members of other racially/ethnically ambiguous groups, like Italians and Greeks. As mentioned in earlier chapters, the US racial stratification system[6] grants certain groups, like Iranians, some flexibility so that they can pass into other groups. Iranians, especially those with lighter phenotypic features like skin color, are hyperaware that they can "phenotypically pass" as other groups like South Americans and Europeans—specifically Italians and Greeks—as well as others from the SWANA region. This sort of racial ambiguity is not necessarily about passing as WASP or northern European but being perceived as a less racialized and stigmatized group, like Italians or Greeks. I asked the interlocutors several questions about who they thought Iranians saw themselves as being most similar and dissimilar to and what racial/ethnic groups they were commonly associated with. Iranians most often cited being mistaken for or perceived as Italian, Greek, Mexican, and South American. One or two said Lebanese and another said Jewish. But very few said they were mistaken for or seen as Iranian, Indian, Turkish, Afghani, or Arab. Seemingly, many Iranians are perceived as being from southern Europe, the Mediterranean region, or a Spanish-speaking country. I argue that these ideas and perceptions[7] have had implications for the coping mechanisms Iranian migrants employ. Experiencing the ability to phenotypically "pass" as Italian, Greek, or South American—being racially flexible[8]—has made racial ambiguity a viable way of protecting oneself against racial profiling and marginal-ization. For example, Nader told me this:

> I think Iranians are lucky because they can sort of slip in. "Okay, you look sort of Italian, you could be sort of close enough." We don't get the same kind of reactions.

Iranians are "lucky," he thought, because their phenotypic features make them racially ambiguous, and they can pass as being Italian. Italians are no longer stigmatized; they are not alien; they have melted into the pot. Iranians are aware that they possess this "racial flexibility," and that they can use ambiguity to their advantage. I asked Nader to further elaborate on his point that Iranians "don't get the same kind of reactions":

> If you sort of wear the hijab, then you will definitely stand out; I imagine you would get more problems.

As opposed to groups who are "too Muslimy," cover their hair, or look stereotypically Middle Eastern, Iranians can pass as southern European. This ambiguity affords them flexibility "to work around" racial/ethnic perceptions and get closer to groups that are less stigmatized and politi-cized than they are. The sentiment that Iranians wish to be seen as a more "benign group," like Italians,[9] was apparent throughout the inter-views. This narrative is so common that a central part of Maz Jobrani's comedic public campaign[10] regarding the 2010 US Census referred to it. The campaign slogan of "check it right; you ain't white" was aimed at encouraging Iranian Americans to mark "other" for race and fill in "Iranian" instead. In the skit, census workers asking Iranians about their race were told to put down "Italian." This sketch reflects the common stereotype of Iranians not wanting to be associated with Iran. It also illustrates the desire for Iranians to remain in the white racial category and their preference for a safer option, like being from "Italy." For exam-ple, Vanessa, a second-generation woman who had grown up and lived in the Bay Area, told me the following about Iran, global politics, and racial/ethnic identity:

> Sometimes I joke with my mom, like, "I wish we were Italian." Everybody loves the Italians. They love their food, they all go there for the summer, and they travel. It's so much happier. And my dad always said, "You know, but Iranians have only been in this country about thirty or so years, it's a newer group. Wait till your kids are grown-ups. It might be easier for them because people are more familiar with the culture and maybe that country has changed a little." And I think when the Chinese came here a long time ago, they were here to build the railroad and there was discrimination towards them . . . or the Irish or even the Italians. And that group has been here for hundreds of years now in the country. So I think once this group has established themselves, I think maybe it'll be easier.

Several significant issues come through in Vanessa's account of how Iranians are currently viewed and where they may be headed. First, she implicitly argues that being Iranian is stigmatizing, so much so that she jokes with her mom of wishing they were perceived in a way like how Italians are perceived. Their ethnicity is symbolic[11] and their culture is known for food, family, and vacationing in their homeland—benign things. This is the opposite of the narrative about Iranians in the last forty years. Vanessa also describes that her father, like many others, believes that Iranians will ultimately follow the path of Europeans. He believes that once Iranians have been in the US longer, have established themselves more deeply into American society and become more familiar to Americans, then Iranians will "melt into the pot." What is more, she told me that Iranians are not "racially different." The differences are mostly cultural, she suggested, and more time spent in the US will bring the two cultures closer together. This expectation, while a common one among Iranians, does not account for the role of larger racial projects or global politics and foreign policy in the racialization and politicization of Iranians in the US. The lack of social citizenship that is often experienced and felt by Iranians is due not to a lack of cultural integration, length of residence, citizenship, or the establishment of communities, organizations, or businesses, but rather to a social and political climate that has persistently racialized Iranians and associated them with violence and terrorism. The experiences of Iranians highlight how racial/ethnic groups can be "simultaneously subjected to processes of whitening and racialization"[12] and how racialization processes occur on a continuum.[13]

Concealment of Identity

Another common coping mechanism is the concealment of identity, which comes in numerous forms. It can entail a shifting away from certain conversations and topics or being reserved about revealing one's racial/ethnic background, and manifest in more tangible and explicit forms, such as changing one's name. Racialization entails the application of meanings not only to phenotype but also language, clothing, and religion—and a name.[14] In Western nations, anglicized names denote a few of the things outlined by Glenn (2002),[15] such as nationality, standing, and allegiance. Adopting such a name signals that one identifies with the culture of that society, that one is a member of it and loyal to it. A name is so powerful that it can shift perceptions, treatment, even opportunity. This type of concealment is common in the US mostly because of racial ambiguity and a degree of "racial flexibility," something not available to Iranians in Germany. The relationship between a name, a sense of familiarity, and employment were reflected in some of Cyrus's experiences in the labor market:

> CYRUS: I have used my name as Brian at work and realized that it worked for me better than my real name and the reason behind that I think is that everybody—the general population—feels a closer relationship in terms of communication. Who you are, and "what we are." I always had to explain what it is, in terms of what I am and who I am. It would always come up.

S: When did you become cognizant that you should or wanted to change your name?

CYRUS: This was around the time I was looking for a job. I was looking for a job around 1993 and I was having a really difficult time and then I realized that maybe that's one thing I could do. I was leaving the oil business, which was international so my name was irrelevant to them, but when I was moving into more domestic work, I notice that this was something I may want to do. At first, I was not getting a lot of callbacks and then that changed.

S: Do you know of any other professionals that do this?

CYRUS: Oh yeah, everybody, a lot of us do this. A lot of Iranians that I know, good number of them, they do this.

S: What does the name change accomplish?

CYRUS: Well, first you do not get trapped with a name like Moham-mad. When you are a doctor, it's like who cares that your name is Mohammad, he is a doctor, he has patients, they are all going to him. But if you are trying to find a job, that is very different.

Several central and interconnected aspects of racialization are made explicit, specifically the negative stigma that is inscribed upon name and ancestry, and the type of limitations that accompany having non-Western attributes and identifiers. Cyrus's use of the word "trap" to describe how non-Western and non-Christian names function in the US labor market is especially noteworthy. A "Muslim name" evokes a set of questions, suspicions, and connotations that counter an applicant's qualifications and skill set. By becoming "Brian" the focus is taken away from Cyrus's racial/ethnic identity, ancestry, and religious background, familiarity is produced, and signals are sent that "he too is an American" and "from here." Ultimately, these alterations did result in callbacks and job interviews. It is noteworthy that this occurred in 1993, during the Gulf War, when the vilification of Arabs and all those perceived as "Arab looking" or "Arab sounding" was high. As illustrated through Cyrus's experiences, Iranians often attempt to escape or ameliorate marginality, discrimination, and racism by making a conscious decision to hide, cover, or withhold parts of their identity. Changing a name is strategically aimed at approximating closeness and familiarity with white Americans and increasing the chances of securing professional opportunities. Cyrus's story also demonstrates that Iranians—including those who have lived in the US for most of their adult lives and have attained advanced educational credentials—must still employ several strategies to ameliorate the discrimination that they face. Like others I spoke with, he also believed that those who have their own private practice or business—like doctors or lawyers—may face less labor market discrimination because they have more freedom and agency, and are respected and valued for their skill set. This is an important point as there are many Iranians, both in the US and Germany, who have become entrepreneurs or started their own businesses because securing work in the labor market was often difficult.[16] Hence, entrepreneurship and small business ownership among first-generation Iranians can be conceived of as a coping mechanism, a response to marginality and discrimination.

Another form of concealing identity is not explicitly revealing or talking about one's racial/ethnic ancestry. This is also a conscious effort on the part of marginalized people, a way to avoid a topic that is expected to cause undue discomfort and potential problems. Paul, a second-generation retired business owner, spoke about his larger relationship to his Iranian and Mexican background:

> You know what? I should say this. Up until I stopped working, I never admitted to that part of my heritage, because there were usually problems associated with that. For example, at my business, we were working on someone's scooter. I had hired my nephew to help me for a summer. For some reason, he brought up the conversation of heritage and the customer heard. I used to have a good rapport with this man, but I could tell in his face that it was, again, fear and loathing, and he never returned.

It would not be until he retired that Paul admitted to having Iranian ancestry. He was upfront about his Mexican ancestry, but his deep awareness and memory of how Iranians were portrayed during the hostage crisis growing up as a teenager had left a lasting impact. These earlier experiences had taught him that he should hide his Iranian heritage. This sense of shame, of not wanting to be identified as Iranian, came to fruition when in passing his nephew mentioned their ancestry in front of a customer who never came back. Paul associated this incident with a larger feeling of "fear and loathing" that Americans hold toward Iranians and others from that part of the world. It was not until he sold his shop and retired that he began to seek out Iranian history and culture. When his economic viability was no longer in danger, he became more comfortable sharing where his father's side of the family was from. Even though self-employment is a means by which one can bypass the formal labor market and not have to worry about being interviewed or promoted, it is not necessarily foolproof. It cannot completely protect one from being treated unfairly. Ultimately, the concealment of identity, anglicization of names, clinging to conceptions of being "Aryan" and racially white, and watering down of cultural and religious values and practices are all means of being less visible and lightening the burden of being racialized and politicized.

While these methods may have lessened the blow of marginality and racism in some ways, the concealment of identity has also, in some ways, been costly for Iranians. The disconnection of the second generation from Iranian culture, mostly because of the first generation's longer-standing problems with the Iranian government, has disconnected some from contemporary Iran and ordinary Iranians. This has influenced some decisions about not visiting Iran and being apprehensive about second-generation Iranians going to Iran. The lack of Persian-language transmission could be another example of this. The other facet of culture that Iranians are often disconnected from is religion, specifically Islam. Iran's theocratic government has had significant impact on Iranians' larger views of politics, religion, and Islam. Seemingly, the first generation's disillusionment with and distrust of politics, along with the turns of political events over the past forty years, has made it hard for some to distinguish between the values of Islam and those who use religion for political gain. Aspects of this may also have been transferred onto the second generation.[17]

Cultural Flexibility and Good and Bad Foreigners

Iranians in Germany cannot melt into a pot, nor are they racially classified as "white," so racial ambiguity, racial flexibility is not available to them. Iranians in Germany are classified as "persons with a migrant background" regardless of generational background or German citizenship. Iranians described how race in Germany is cultural but also deeply rooted in specific phenotypic attributes, like fair skin color, blond hair, and blue eyes. This phenotypic specificity does not exist in the US in the same way; it is not just the "Nordic races" or "Aryans" who are considered white, and this matters a great deal in what kind of racial flexibility is and is not available in each context. By this definition of whiteness and German-ness, Iranians cannot pass into being German. What is available to them is being "good foreigners." Often Iranians express the feeling that they receive a more positive reception than other foreigners, because Germans see them as willing to adopt German values and norms and change certain aspects of their cultural outlooks and practices. Iranians were the kind of foreigners that were "capable of striking this balance," because they were "culturally flexible" and less rooted in "traditional ways of thinking and living."

Who are "good foreigners" and what do they look like? As will be shown, they are those who mix and mingle with Germans and German organizations; find German friends and even dating partners and mates; adhere to secularism and democratic ideals (freedom of expression, freedom of the press); abide by the rules and regulations of German society; are punctual, disciplined, and organized; learn the German language quickly; and avoid living in areas and neighborhoods that are populated by non-Germans. Numerous conversations revealed a deeply held belief among Iranians that they are good foreigners because of the Iranian community's successful integration. For the most part, Iranians believe that they are treated more positively than others, especially Turks, because of the community's tendency to be educated, secular, and self-employed. As I will show, "cultural flexibility" is manifested in the analysis and discussion of two responses to being racialized, the "good and bad foreigners" trope and *beweisen* (proving yourself).

When Hormuz, a first-generation professional who had migrated to Germany and received his PhD in the early 1970s, was asked about whether Germany prefers some migrants over others, he asserted that Germans prefer immigrants with skills, and this is the reason why Iranians are accepted. He told me that Iranians do not "give Germany any trouble," meaning that Iranians are willing to culturally assimilate and/or integrate. They quickly learn German, adopt German customs and norms, and do not "abuse the social welfare programs" compared to other foreigners, like Turks. Accordingly, if a foreigner experiences marginality and discrimination, they are likely responsible for it in some way.

Iranians commonly recite the hegemonic narratives about Turks in German society, the same ones espoused by German politicians, policy makers, intellectuals, and the press. Iranians often describe "bad foreigners" as being visibly religious (read Muslim), living in mainly immigrant neighborhoods and ethnic enclaves, working in service-sector occupations, lacking German-language fluency, "feeding off" the social welfare system, not socially mixing with Germans in the public or private sphere, and having no respect for the culture or the rules and regulations of German society. Consequently, these individuals cannot properly succeed in Germany, the story goes, because they have refused to integrate into German society. These distinctions regarding culture and religion come through in Lailea's account of how migrants are received in Germany:

> It depends on who the immigrant is. If the immigrant is liberal and open to German culture, it's easier for them to be accepted. But let's say—I

know a girl who is Arab, she wears a headscarf and also speaks with an accent—and that is very difficult for Germans to accept. It's like, "Look how she is talking and is living here in Germany." You can't speak like that in Germany. Deep inside, I think that Germans still have some anti-foreigner feelings; they still have ill feelings toward foreigners.

Foreigners are marginalized because they are not liberal enough. Although Lailea argues that Germany remains a non-immigrant-accepting society and continues to harbor "ill feelings toward foreigners," she also believes that there is a hierarchy—some foreigners are more accepted than others. The "good foreigners" are more tolerated because they are *liberal* and open to German culture and values. Conversely, foreigners who visibly display that they are Muslim are placed in the unacceptable or "bad foreigner" category, because it is assumed they are "illiberal" and "traditional." Lailea went on to explain why Iranians are seen as "good foreigners" compared to Arabs or Turks:

> I don't ever see Iranians wearing headscarves; it's mostly Turks that wear them. Iranians dress well, are pretty, dance, laugh, and Germans like that about us. They think, "They are like Europeans, they're not too Muslim. They eat pepperoni pizza as well." The Muslim thing is important in Germany because it's different and it's strange to them. We drink our wine, smoke our cigarettes, dance, we wear makeup, they see us as being similar to them, and then we are a bit exotic. Turks sit there and say, "We won't eat pork, we won't drink, we won't dance to this, we pray and go to the mosque, we praise our own culture," and sometimes they don't even know one word of German.

Supposedly, several things make Iranians more acceptable than other foreigners. Iranians are not too religious, "very Muslim," or strongly rooted in traditional Iranian practices and customs. This is illustrated by Lailea's statement that Iranians will "eat pepperoni pizza . . . drink our wine, smoke our cigarettes." In these instances, Iranians are culturally closer to Germans and appear "less foreign" because they are "culturally flexible." Lailea considers Iranians to be malleable and more culturally "fit and able" to become a part of German society because they are not weighed down by tradition and do not allow their cultural or religious background to impede integration. Azad, a second-generation man, also emphasized how cultural differences influence integration among immigrant communities:

> There are people that adopt and try to blend into society; they are perceived as the ones that are helpful and, normally, they don't have any problems in Germany. But there are also groups of immigrants that are, you know, for example the Turkish, who very much like their culture and try to hold on to it. They build up this cultural wall. They look down on Germans because they believe that they know nothing of honor. For example, they may say something like this about a German woman or Western woman: "She had a boyfriend before me, that's a problem, and she is not marriage material." . . . They separate each other from the whole society with this.

Like Hormuz, Azad contends that foreigners will not have problems in Germany if they accept and adopt German values and norms, do not "segregate themselves" from Germans, and do not "cling" to their ethnic culture. He also makes an indirect distinction between those foreigners who are perceived as being helpful and "build bridges" compared to those who "build walls" between themselves and Germans. Azad's narrative falls within the popular discourse about Turks in Germany—namely, that they are traditional, religious, and shun certain things, like casual dating or having sex before marriage. Lailea's description of Iranians as being "more liberal and accepting of German culture" is related to Azad's comment that immigrants create problems for themselves by not "blending [with] and adopting" German culture. Unlike Iranians, Turks are seen as not possessing this "cultural flexibility"; they are unwilling to adapt to German cultural values and norms and thus are to an extent to blame for their marginality. Iranians are cognizant of how they are often perceived by Germans and how foreigners in general are perceived, and seem to actively attempt to downplay attributes and characteristics that could disadvantage them in German society.

It is also worth pointing out how gender affects conversations around integration;[18] for Iranian women, racial difference does not evoke fear but often makes them "exotic"[19] and interesting. The idea that Iranian and other Middle Eastern women are "exotic" and thus attractive to Westerners, especially white men, was pronounced in both Germany and the US. In some instances, Iranian women believed this to be a compliment, something that works in their favor, while others find it offensive. In my conversations with Iranian women who had dated or were married to German men, some explicitly cited physical attractiveness and family culture as factors that made them more desirable than German women. For example, they argued that Iranian women looked more feminine, dressed up more, were more "put together," and showered German men "with an abundant amount of love and affection," which was something rare to them. Iranian culture was also seen as "more fun and livelier" compared to German culture; the claim that "marriage with Iranian women loosens up German men" is something I heard often. Also, it cannot be denied that Iranian women benefit, in some ways, when they marry or start a family with German men.[20] Some of the Iranian women I spoke with argued that marrying Germans offers a kind of "deeper integration," as it makes life in Germany relatively easier, both socially and economically, especially if you have children. For example, Pooneh, a first-generation Iranian woman, argued that marrying a German man was not only an opportunity to appreciate German culture in a deeper, more intimate way, but also a chance to "free" herself from some of the constraints that being Iranian in Germany may produce. Anahita, whose experiences I shared in the previous chapter, offered a description of being immersed in German social circles, including friends and romantic partners, that vividly demonstrates this. While her thoughts had recently changed on the matter,[21] she told me this about dating and romantic partners:

> There was a time where I only wanted to date a German man, because I thought I would be able to situate myself well within this society. I have always been the type of person that has wanted to place myself well in this society and most of the decisions that I've made have been based on that. The way I have chosen my friends is how I wanted to choose my partner.

Anahita was deeply mindful of the importance of "situating herself"[22] within German society and had always picked her friends "strategically." Aside from Iranian cousins, she did not have friends of foreign background until she attended university. Like Pooneh, she felt that being in German circles is a way to maneuver through German culture and gain insight and familiarity with it. In her twenties, she mostly wanted to date German men because of this. Notably, the Iranian men I spoke with who had German female partners did not necessarily see their lives improving in the same ways as Iranian women who had German male partners.[23]

As I have shown, the "good foreigners" trope is born out of experiences of racialization and marginality, and it is a coping mechanism by which Iranians attempt to disassociate with unintegrated migrants—the "bad foreigners." The idea of an honorary, quintessential "good foreigner" category helps facilitate distance from the "bad foreigners," the immigrants who lack integration and are associated with unskilled work. This trope allows some Iranians to symbolically distance themselves from those who are deemed "worse off" and temporarily feel better about their position as perpetual foreigners in Germany. Given the existing racial order and hierarchies, whether racial and/or cultural, non-Germans must fit somehow and that fitting almost always entails some downplaying or covering aspects of identity that signal "foreignness." It also often means socializing with Germans and having German friendship and work networks as a means of expressing cultural proximity and securing cultural, social, and economic capital.[24] I maintain that labeling oneself and being wanted to be seen as "one of the good ones" is meant to ameliorate feelings of alienation and marginality, this feeling of being less than.

Beweisen (Proving Yourself)

Through symbolic and cultural appeals, Iranians aim to signal that they are culturally closer to Germans compared to other foreigners, especially newly arriving ones from Syria, Afghanistan, and Iraq. This boundary between "good and bad foreigners" is explicit in the popular discourse that Turks, Muslims, and other foreigners are "difficult" and unwilling to adopt German values and practices, but instead "use and abuse" state social insurance programs and prefer a "Germany without Germans." The 2016 follow-up interviews revealed an increased effort on the part of Iranians to "prove"[25] to Germans that they are integrated and "the good foreigners." This was often subtle and involved some signaling to Germans that Iranians were more like them than the new foreigners. As outlined in the previous chapter, since the refugee crisis interactions with Germans had gotten more tense and Iranians felt these shifts. For example, when I asked Isabel about her exchanges with Germans, she responded:

> ISABEL: It is implicit. I try to prove to them I'm like them in more
> implicit ways. For example, me and my dog, and when I say that my
> dog is my baby and how I talk to my dog, and then they say, "Well, in
> your cultures I didn't think you like dogs or you'd be this close with
> animals," and I'd say, "No, this is my baby."
> S: What does the symbol of the dog hold? What does having a dog say?
> ISABEL: "Okay, she is not a Muslim. Those who are Muslim, they walk
> away or distance themselves from dogs."
> S: Is it just about religion or is it culture and tradition too?
> ISABEL: Germans see it as a religious thing, as Islam.

Isabel's reaction to the changing climate is to find ways to signal to Germans that she is culturally like them; her love of dogs reduces the social distance between her and Germans, given the role that dogs play in German society.[26] What this also reveals is that the preference for dogs in Germany is not necessarily seen as a cultural or traditional matter, but rather is seen as religion based. According to this logic, Muslims, and Islam more generally, are not accepting of dogs. The commentary about dogs is similar to the earlier discussion surrounding eating pork. Foreigners, especially Middle Eastern or Muslim, are more socially accepted if they eat pork than if they do not. This sentiment is directly connected to Lailea's comment in the 2011 interview that Iranians are not as "traditional" and will drink a glass of wine or eat pepperoni on their pizza. These actions "prove" to Germans that Iranians' lifestyle preferences are not dictated by the religious or cultural customs of their homeland, that they have fully integrated themselves into German society and feel themselves to be German. The expectation that foreigners prove their "cultural fitness" by being malleable and willing to integrate Western and Christian ideals, values, and practices speaks to the ethnocultural dimensions of social citizenship and belonging.

Another form of proving oneself is in the form of "correcting" newly received refugees on "proper etiquette" in public spaces, in front of Germans. My conversations brought up interesting stories of Iranians intervening to "correct" foreigners in public. This included cautioning foreigners to not talk on their phones, eat food while using public transportation, or speak non-German loudly in public, and telling foreign men that "German women dress like this, but that does not mean you can stare at them." Seemingly, many Iranians feel that their fate in Germany is tied to how well new refugees "appear" to have integrated. Some Iranians felt it important to remind foreigners what kind of society they had been admitted into. This is quite clear in Buye Gandom's recounting of her dealings with refugees:

> Me, also being a foreigner, I may allow myself to tell them that eating here is prohibited, that you cannot talk loudly on your phone, but a German would never do this.

When I asked her why she feels the need to intervene, she stated that:

> I do not want my image to be tarnished, because I see how Germans are looking and how they perceive this. I also do it because I hope that they learn. It's like, okay, you want to live here, but you must adjust to German society; it's not like we're in Iran where everyone is talking loudly, screaming, talking over each other. . . . When I interject, it's good for me, because I do not want to get on the train tomorrow and have them say that all foreigners are rotten, to have our image tarnished.

For Buye Gandom, public interventions help save and maintain the reputation that Iranians have created for themselves in Germany. It shows Germans that not all "foreigners are the same," while also teaching newcomers the socially and culturally appropriate ways of behaving in Germany. To "become good foreigners," newly arriving refugees will have to learn to quickly adapt to the values, norms, and practices of German society. If the new refugees do not learn to adapt to German cultural values and norms, then tomorrow the image of all foreigners will be "tarnished." This broader discourse that new refugees are a threat to social position and can "make it bad for us" is centered on existing racial/cultural differentiation and stratification within Germany. Given that most Iranians see themselves as an integrated and relatively successful immigrant community, being lumped together with foreigners who are seen as unintegrated creates "problems" as well as anxiety. They understand the challenges and difficulties of living in a society that maintains anti-foreigner prejudice and racism, but also expect newcomers to integrate quickly and become less "visibly foreign" and "less Muslim." It is assumed that the new refugees will make it "bad for everyone" if they don't quickly adapt, resulting in further stigmatization, racialization, and marginality.

The interviews also make clear that throughout Germany and Europe Islam continues to be articulated as an antithesis to progress, civility, and modernity, and Iranians believe that being secular, or appearing so, will result in better treatment in Germany. This is not much different than the post-9/11 climate in the US, where Muslims are persistently marginalized, racially profiled, and even demonized for practicing Islam. This anti-Muslim racism was quite evident in the public and political discourse that emerged after New Year's Eve 2015, in which Arab and Muslim men were described as attacking innocent women because they were violent and "sexually repressed." In this larger social climate, as I have shown, Iranians have adopted several coping mechanisms to work around their racialization and marginality. These include attempts at racial ambiguity, concealment of identity, and gestures aimed at proving themselves to be "good foreigners." The racial stratification systems in the US and Germany produce the possibilities, conditions, and mechanisms through which these coping strategies and "racial flexibility" in the US and "cultural flexibility" in Germany are produced and expressed.

Racialized Belonging

I have shown how racialization and racial othering have led Iranians to a variety of responses in their attempts to navigate and ameliorate marginality. My argument thus far has also been that racialization and politicization has been an impediment to Iranians experiencing belonging in the US and Germany. In the United States, Iranians often cite Iran's political relationship with the United States and the rise of anti-immigrant, anti–Middle Eastern, and anti-Muslim racism as the cause of their marginalization. In some instances, Iranians feel profiled because they are non-white immigrants; other times they were marginalized because they were presumed to be Arab or Muslim. In many others, they cite the unresolved issues between the US and Iran as a major source. They referred to the pre-revolutionary years as a time of better relations, of days when Iranians received positive treatment in the US. Iranians entertained what ifs: "what if the relationship between the US and Iran were to be better," or "what if there was diplomacy between them again." Many in the Iranian American community believe that they will be treated better and will cease to be looked upon as "enemies" if, and when, diplomacy between the nations improves. In this sense, they saw their ability to belong as inextricably tied to global politics, not to their being foreigners or immigrants.

The US and Germany continue to use racial thinking in both discourse and policy, domestically and globally. This means that is not possible for those racialized to erase race or its impact or implications. Rather, they can cope, manage, and maneuver the racial system by "doing their best" to appeal to dominant myths and expectations in the hopes of approximate belonging, or getting as close as possible. I consider "conditional belonging" as involving a set of conditions and qualifications that must be fulfilled and certain attributes that must be erased and eradicated[27] before one can feel like an equal member of society. In the following pages, I consider how cumulative experiences of discrimination, marginality, and racialization have led Iranians to experience "conditional belonging."

Conditional Belonging

Levitt and Schiller (2004) conceptualize "being" as the ability to partake in institutions, organizations, experiences, and cultural practices on various levels, yet not identify with, or belong to these institutions, organizations, experiences, or cultural practices. I consider "being" to be a form of "conditional belonging." Conditional belonging speaks to the salience of race and the role it plays in social citizenship and membership in Western nations, where the attainment of "unconditional belonging" remains racially rooted and based.

Belonging is subjective and unstable; it can and does change. Often, belonging is in flux and shaped by perceptions, feelings, and experiences. I asked the interlocutors questions about what they thought belonging was, and what it felt like. Cyrus explained:

Belonging is a very high level of qualification. And I don't think belonging is a one-way street; it's a two-way street, and in that sense, I don't think belonging is really there. We are trying to penetrate this society in a way that we can lead comfortable lives, that's my view. The situation is that you are trying to get acceptance so you can have a comfortable life; you don't belong here per se in that regard. Belonging means all the avenues and all the parts of society are working for you.

Belonging is something that is deeply felt, and entails that all parts of the society, system, and culture are working for you, that you have equal participation. It means that you are a politically and economically integrated and included and represented in the dominant culture. Belonging would also mean that Iranian Americans would not be associated with the actions of the Iranian government, would not be racialized and politicized because of it. They would be able to create their own narrative and advance a more realistic representation of the Iranian American community in the US. While Iranians have not achieved this level, Cyrus believes that the belonging of Iranians is still "a work in progress"; Iranians are working to enter, integrate, and create a comfortable life for themselves and their families. But "unconditional belonging" is not there, yet. Tony, a first-generation immigrant man living in northern California, said the following about what would help him experience belonging:

> If the relationship between Iran and the US was like before. That would definitely make a big difference, because then there would be no clash.

Tony had lived in the US since the late 1970s and spoke to me on two occasions, in 2011 and 2018. The "clash" that makes it hard for Iranians to experience belonging is mostly about the political relationship between the US and Iran over the last forty years. Iranians feel forever burdened by the associations that are made between ordinary Iranians and the actions of the Iranian government. In her 2017 interview, Siv also spoke about Iran-US relations and belonging. She elaborated on Tony's point about "the big difference" that positive Iran-US relations would have on the lives of Iranians by talking about comfort and happiness:

> I think I would be happier. All of us would be happier if Iran had a good reputation. I think it would bring us more prestige. I think a lot of people would be more comfortable saying they're Iranian. I mean the whole concept of Persian and Iranian came from the fact that Iranians here were not comfortable saying they were Iranian. They say "Persian" so people think about Persian carpets and Persian Empire, and don't confuse that with Iran.

Siv makes several notable points that connect the social and political climate to feelings of belonging, shame, and discomfort and the concealing of one's identity. One is that the narrative of Iran being a part of an "Axis of Evil" and "terrorist sponsoring," the Muslim Ban, and the uncertainty of the political relationship between Iran and the United States impacts Iranians' happiness and comfort. In a climate of being racialized, politically stigmatized, and targeted by the Muslim Ban, Iranians cannot be themselves, but rather work on concealing their identity. Second, she mentions that Iranians aim to "confuse" Americans about their racial/ethnic identity by using the term "Persian," that this is a conscious effort on their part, a way to maneuver out of a potentially uncomfortable conversation or exchange. This is a topic that is discussed among Iranians; there is even some division in the community about what the term "Persian" refers to, how it should be used, and whether the distinction of "Persian" makes much sense outside of Iran. Siv's point that Iranians would rather Americans think of "Persian carpets" and the "Persian Empire," instead of anything related to Iran, is a common sentiment. Even Americans who are familiar with Iranians often curiously ask, "What is the difference between Persian and Iranian? Why do some use one over the other?" Siv underscores how belonging is mediated by the larger social and political climate and context, and that marginality and discrimination is antithetical to experiencing unconditional belonging.

Nick was also one of the respondents who felt that changes in the so-cial and political climate, specifically the rise of white nationalism in the US, had caused him to doubt his place in the US. Despite his having been in the US since he was a young adult, for over forty years, he told me:

> All these people saying stuff they couldn't say before, all these white su-premacist and white people saying all these things. No matter how long I stay in this country, I'm still a minority. As soon as I open my mouth, they say, "You are from somewhere else."

The explicit nature of anti-immigrant and anti-Muslim prejudice and racism after the election of Trump is a consistent theme throughout the follow-up interviews with Iranians. They told me that white Americans had been granted permission by the POTUS to talk and behave in rac-ist ways; they were repeating his words, his hatred. Decades had passed since they had felt this worried, scared, and unsafe in the US. For Nick, who experienced trauma throughout the late 1970s and early 1980s, this reemergence of racism was not only worrisome but made him feel like an "outsider" all over again—after over forty years, he was still a minority, he still lacked unconditional belonging, his belonging was conditional. The conditions were based on Iranians not speaking a for-eign language in public, not phenotypically looking "brown, Muslim, or Arab," appearing culturally Western, and also going below the radar and becoming "undetectable."

While race/ethnicity—being non-white—is mentioned at times as the reason for marginality and stigmatization, Iranians in the US also regard global political factors as being a central aspect of their racialization and political stigmatization. This leads some to say that if the reputation of Iran, and by extension Iranians, were to improve than they would be treated more fairly, like equal members of American society. It is the idea of the US as a nation of immigrants, a color-blind nation where one's religious or racial/ethnic background does not impact opportunity and success, that drives Iranians' assessments of the role of race and ancestry in the US.

In Germany, "conditional belonging" shows up in the notion that one will "always be a foreigner." As I highlighted in the previous chapter, Iranians directly name ancestry as the reason for why they cannot belong; a real German has German ancestry. This is in stark contrast to Iranians in the US, who very seldom argue that America is a white nation and that one can belong only via being or passing as white. The experience of "conditional belonging," was quite vivid among second-generation Iranians. For example, when I asked Ismael about belonging, he started with:

> There are some things that make me feel like I'm totally a part of this society. Then there are some of the experiences that I've had that are linked to having dark hair or being a foreigner. I can be wearing the nicest clothing and they can still tell me that you cannot come in, that we cannot let you in. These things make me feel frustrated and upset me.

Ismael told me that being born in Germany and having lived there his entire life, speaking fluent German, having German friends, having gone to school including college, working, and participating in German cultural practices all made him feel there was nothing different about him. These are the things that made him feel like he belonged. But it was his race/ethnicity that had limited his employment opportunities, led him to be treated differently and discriminated against in public spaces, including bars and nightclubs. In many ways he had been made to feel perpetually foreign externally—this was not something of his own doing. Houshang had been in Germany since the early 1970s and had established a comfortable life for himself and his family. He considered himself well integrated in German society, and when I asked him about belonging, he told me:

> It's that thing that remains hidden in German people, it's that Germans will not accept you as a foreigner. The feeling that I got in Canada was

not that they said this person is a foreigner, this person is an insider, and this person is a Canadian. I did not get that sense from people there. I saw that an Indian man was wearing a turban but was a policeman there; here in the offices you do not see that, in any public jobs you will not see that. Six million non-Germans live here, but you see them less in public jobs, in government, public jobs. And it is these things, when you are not accepted in this society, you sense that you are not a part of that society. When a foreigner or an Iranian comes to the US, they say, "My America"; no one here will say, "My Germany!" I have this fight with Germans constantly: you guys pay a lot of our social expenses, set up schools for us, give us asylum and residency, but the feeling that I am a part of you, you do not give us that feeling, that emotion does not exist.

Houshang feels that the years spent in Germany do not translate into the German people giving immigrants the feeling that they are a part of Germany. Yes, the German state provides institutional resources for state asylum and resettlement resources, but German society remains unwelcoming toward foreigners. Houshang also points out that public and state occupations remain exclusionary toward foreigners; unlike places like Canada and the US that have truly integrated racial/ethnic minorities, Germany is still lagging on true inclusion. In the US and Canada, you can wear a veil to work because it is protected by the law, as opposed to Germany, which still has not adopted such norms of racial/ethnic and religious pluralism. He also kept pointing out the subjective aspects of belonging—it is a "feeling," a sense of being "an insider"—and that Germans do not give or express this feeling to foreigners, even those who have been there for decades.

Iranians repeatedly mentioned this idea that "no matter how long you have lived amongst Germans, no matter how long they have known you, they can turn on you and fall back into their anti-foreigner leanings." This sentiment had become especially profound since the 2015 refugee crisis. Kasra, a second-generation man, said this when I asked about belonging:

You try all your life to integrate, but you're always a foreigner and then you think, "What is different about me?" That's the hard thing, it's painful; it's made me suffer greatly. There are few people that I have talked to the way I talked to you. These discussions must be had. People say that Muslims, Iranians, Arabs won't integrate, but you won't let us. That is the problem that is the main problem. So many books are written that Muslims, foreigners, that "their lives don't match ours, they don't open up to our society." But it doesn't matter; no matter how much you try, the Germans won't let it.

Kasra continued:

I feel that every foreigner, Iranian and Turks, have this feeling of being foreigners, and that they will always be foreigners. . . . There are a lot of them that have given up. Many of them have repressed this, and sometimes it comes out, people just implode. When they see that their friends, friends that have always been their friends, close friends, are only friends because he/she never discussed this with them, because they have censored themselves. And this situation is a problem that exists a lot.

Like Cyrus in the US, Kasra also argues that belonging requires both sides to participate equally. Germans must be willing to accept foreigners not just as refugees and asylum seekers—people in need of humanitarian aid—but rather as equal members of German society who are afforded the same treatment and opportunities as the native German population. Germans will have to stop acting like foreigners are "guests" or "belong somewhere else" and start seeing Iranians and other immigrant communities as people who contribute to society, that pay taxes, and add to the culture, values, and diversity of German society. When I asked Pari about belonging she explained that, after three-plus decades, there was still something lacking. She described it like this:

If I were to get that emotional warmth from Germans, I would sense that belonging here. If a German were to look at me and say, "You've been with us for thirty-seven years, I hope that you are happy with us here, living here." But a German would say, "You've been here for thirty-seven years? Have you considered going back?" That's the difference.

Pari had been in Germany for thirty-seven years, but the lingering anti-foreigner racism in German society, which prevents immigrants from sensing membership and "warmth," had kept her from feeling that Germany was her home. She provided an example of how "feeling wanted" in Germany could look like, but her lived experiences had shown her that instead of being seen as an asset, as participating members of German society, foreigners are mostly seen as a burden. These kinds of narratives are frequent among Iranians living in Germany, and even middle-class professionals cannot escape this sense of not feeling fully wanted in German society. The implications this has for belonging and social membership is clear—one cannot feel "unconditional belonging" in a society where one is treated like a perpetual guest that should one day "go back to where they came from."

In Germany, Iranians find it hard to believe that "unconditional belonging" is attainable. Unlike Iranians in the US, they felt the deep-rooted nature of descent-based belonging and social membership and did not expect to belong. There is no national narrative of being "color-blind" or a "land of immigrants" for Iranians to attach to, internalize, or utilize. The recognition that one may never "shed" foreign ancestry, never be seen as or treated like a German, no matter how long you live in Germany, was also hard to come to terms with, especially among second-generation Iranians. Anti-foreigner racism is also perceived as pervasive, omnipresent, and continuously impacting the ability to belong. Iranians in Germany perceive that they will never be able to proudly declare that Germany is their nation; rather they feel like perpetual guests and foreigners in Germany. It is anti-foreigner racism—not Iranians' lack of integration—that impedes belonging. Given that unconditional belonging is exclusive, mechanisms and responses are developed to approximate it.

Being a "good foreigner" is ultimately meant to ameliorate feelings of conditional belonging and perpetual foreignness. For some, the denial that anti-foreigner prejudice and racism is centrally rooted in descent/race-based definitions of German national identity and community serves an emotional function. In other words, Iranians may be passed up for work and opportunities, yet at least they can find solace in the belief that their group does not stick to tradition or "religious conservatism." And at least, when Iranians do practice their culture, they do it in an "acceptable" manner—they know what aspects of their culture to highlight and which ones to downplay when the occasion requires it. In some ways, then, Iranians display and perform culture safely and cautiously, without rocking the boat. As I have argued, these coping mechanisms—becoming good foreigners, proving oneself, concealing identity—are all made possible through a certain degree of racial or cultural flexibility that Iranians possess in each context.

Discussion

This chapter's objective has been to show the cumulative impact of several layered and interwoven factors that produce feelings of conditional belonging and perpetual foreignness. The interview data from both 2010–2011 and 2016–2018 draw our attention to a significant social boundary between Germans and foreigners. Germany's conception of belonging and identity remains tied to the *Volk* and is based on ancestry and phenotype. The boundaries drawn between native Germans and foreigners are based on racial/ethnic ancestry, culture, and religion. Being an *Ausländer* means never becoming a true German; the closest one comes to being German is as a "plastic Deutsch" or a German with a passport, a naturalized foreigner. Charles Mills's (1999) argument that the notion of liberalism that is promoted in Western liberal nations is a racialized (white) liberalism where whiteness is a prerequisite for the attainment of individualism, equal rights, and citizenship is reflected in the narratives and stories of immigrant and second-generation respondents who possessed a racialized perception of German identity, national membership, and belonging. They overwhelmingly believed that the protections of citizenship, equal rights, and social citizenship were something that only Germans could unconditionally attain.

The comparative case presented in this book makes clear that in nations like the US and Germany—where race and ancestry were historically integral aspects of belonging and social membership—unconditional belonging is unavailable to nonmembers despite their attainment of conventional measures of integration. In the US, Iranians experience being watched and treated with suspicion because they are identified as being from Iran and stereotyped as being loyal to the Iranian state. The racialization of Iranians in Germany is more explicitly about nationality and standing. Oftentimes foreigners are treated as if they are incapable of being like members of their host society, because they lack the right culture, the right ancestry, etc. The similarities and differences in the experiences of Iranians are rooted in the attributes of each nation, racial history, and how race operates in each social and political context.

Moreover, the dominant narrative in Western nations like the US and Germany, that immigrants, refugees, or racial/ethnic minorities will be accepted "once" they attain a certain level of cultural and structural integration through the attainment of educational and professional credentials is not reflected in my conversations with Iranians in either nation. Iranians in both contexts were overwhelmingly college educated and fluent in English and German. They possess legal residency and citizenship, are secular, and reside in predominately white and German-majority neighborhoods. By the prevailing measures of integration, Iranians are very well integrated. But this does not necessarily guarantee social citizenship and unconditional belonging in nations with deeply entrenched racial systems and structures. Immigrant integration, while important in securing social and economic mobility, cannot undo legacies of racism, racial systems, racial projects, racial thinking, and processes of racialization.

This comparative research also highlights how the institutional arrangements in each nation, and the differences among them, affect the extent to which Iranians can secure higher-level academic credentials and professional opportunities and positions. Institutionalized state refugee policy and social insurance is provided by nations like Germany, yet migrant populations and their children, when compared to the native German population, still face barriers in accessing vocational programs, the academic education tracks, and professional job opportunities. In the interviews, first- and second-generation Iranian immigrants spoke of educational tracking and the difficulties in securing higher-level academic credentials and professional employment and advancement. In the US, Iranians face different institutional arrangements, which means they are more able to create middle-class and upper-middle-class lives. This, in part, signals to Iranians that, despite their ongoing racialization and politicization, upward mobility and the American Dream are still feasible and that it is only a matter of time before they can access unconditional belonging and social membership.

Examining the experiences of Iranians in the two nations also underscores how racial stratification systems and processes of racialization are organized in the US and Germany, how they influence and shape racial classification, and how the racial and cultural boundaries in each place dictate and mediate how Iranians have coped, managed, and responded to racialization and marginality. In Germany, Iranians are not considered racially white, are not racially flexible, and being an *Ausländer* is not something that is shed within one or two generations. The options available to Iranians in the US—to be racially malleable and have situational access to whiteness—are not available to Iranians in Germany. Iranians attempt to circumvent racialization and marginality through culturally flexibility, by becoming "good foreigners," or "quintessential foreigners," through making cultural and symbolic appeals. This includes acculturating to and actively adopting German culture, values, characteristics, and practices and working to prove to Germans that they are not "bad foreigners" and thus worthy of equal and fair treatment.

Being racially ambiguous or being able to pass into being German is not available to Iranians and other immigrant populations in Germany, and "unconditional belonging" and social citizenship remain race- and ancestry-based. The racialization and politicization of Iranians in the US is mostly about their homeland, or the homeland of their parents and the wider political conflicts in the Middle East and Muslim-majority nations. Ongoing racial projects and larger global politics have created an unwelcoming environment for Iranians in the US, making it difficult for them to attain a better quality of life, have equal access to opportunities and resources in society, and experience belonging. Some attempt to cope with and manage racialization and marginality through the concealment of identity and cultivation of racial ambiguity. The experiences of Iranians in the US illustrate the "racialization process continuum"[28] and reflect the existing racial stratification system in the country. That is, Iranians are granted a degree of racial ambiguity, racial flexibility, and social membership; however, their experiences of racism, discrimination, and marginality place them outside of whiteness,[29] highlighting the liminal and shifting nature of their "honorary white" racial status and the precarity of belonging.

Conclusion

As I sit here writing concluding thoughts, it has been announced that Donald Trump has not been reelected. I have more questions than answers: "Is it finally over? What is in store for Iran and Iranians? Now that Trump has been defeated, is there a possibility of a rekindling of the Iran Deal? Are there better days to come for Iranian families separated by sanctions and travel restrictions, for those struggling under a crippling Iranian economy? What is to come under the Biden administration? Will relations get better or worse?"

President Biden repealed Executive Order 13780 (Protecting the Nation from Foreign Terrorist Entry into the United States), the second version of Trump's Muslim Ban, on January 20, 2021. Now what will become of the 2015 Iran Nuclear Deal? Will the US and Europe get back to the table for negotiations? That is very uncertain as the talks that began in Vienna on November 29, 2021, with the newly elected Iranian government, the United States, Britain, China, France, Germany, and Russia have so far not gone well. The Iranian government has asked for the immediate removal of all sanctions imposed under Trump, lifting the designation of the Islamic Revolutionary Guard Corps (IRGC) as a terrorist organization, and a guarantee that no future US administration would withdraw from the deal again. There has also been talk that the Biden administration may tighten economic sanctions yet further. However, it is unclear whether further sanctions would deter the Iranian government from uranium enrichment given that Iran has continued with its program despite those sanctions already in place.[1] There has also been talk of targeting Iran's oil sales to China and the United Arab Emirates. Some believe that even war is not off the table.[2]

Most recently, talks between Iran and European Union officials in February and March 2022 yielded little sign that the 2015 deal will be revived, and prospects are growing increasingly dim.[3] While the Trump administration's "maximum pressure" campaign of imposing increased sanctions against Iran was supposedly meant to achieve an "improved deal," it failed to produce any such result.[4] What the ramifications will be if the Iran Nuclear Deal is not revived are still unclear, but the consequences of foreign policy and global political relations are as critical as they were in the late 1970s and early 1980s.

Decades ago, Said (1997) argued that the ways we conceptualize and talk about those that practice Islam and people from Iran and surrounding regions have a great impact on both American popular culture and foreign policy. This impact was evident in the experiences of Iranians who participated in this research. They spoke of an undeniable shift in their experiences during the Obama administration compared to the Trump era. They argued that policies aimed at further isolating Iran from the global political community caused them to fear for their safety in the US. Many openly wondered about what might happen to them and their families if war between the US and Iran became a reality. While Iranians in Western countries have legal status, are citizens, attained educational credentials, and achieved some economic mobility, they cite heightened experiences of fear, threat, and exclusion, and they worry greatly about the communities' future in these nations. For many, the question of what will happen to Iran and the Iranian people in the coming years remains a matter of great unease. There is growing anxiety that the Iran Deal will never be rekindled. This is of special concern to those who have family members living in Iran and Iranian dual nationals who know and experience first-hand how foreign policy relations between Iran and Western nations affect the lives of everyday Iranians. The ability to travel to and from Iran to visit family, to study or work internationally, to buy or invest in property, or to visit Iran as a tourist are all predicated upon diplomatic relations between Iran and the West. It is the continued hope of many Iranians living within and outside Iran that the global political tensions that have impacted them and their families for forty-plus years will be resolved one day.

Nativism in the US and across Europe, and the revitalization of explicit narratives of "Wir sind das Volk"[5] (We are the people), "Germany for the Germans," "Reclaim America,"[6] "Make America Great Again," and "the Reconquest"[7] were also of great concern for Iranians. They believed that these slogans and the policies that accompany them had hardened the line between "who belongs" and "who does not belong," increasing their apprehension about what the social and political climate in the US and Germany would look like in coming years. The rise of racial nationalism underscores the unresolved racisms of Western nations and demonstrates a fundamental shift from a covert form of racism, where exclusion was hidden in a larger narrative of color-blindness, liberal democracy, and humanitarianism, toward an overt form of racism toward immigrants, refugees, and asylum seekers coming from the Global South. These movements will not only perpetuate the racialization of non-white communities—negatively affecting their lives socially, politically, and materially—but will also further increase the racial/ethnic and religious dimensions of social belonging, membership, and social citizenship. Given these larger movements and shifts in the social and political climate, is Germany truly willing to accept that it is becoming religiously plural and multi-racial/ethnic? Will it fulfill its promises of being a humanitarian and liberal society? And how do those of Iranian heritage live in a culture and system that still seemingly does not want them there, that treats them like *Ausländers* and perpetual guests, even after decades of residence? The same sort of questions can be asked of the United States. Will the US continue to strive to be what it calls itself, a "nation of immigrants," a place that is "color-blind" and where people of all backgrounds are equally welcomed and protected, or will it follow a different course? Will we continue to see support for racial nationalism, anti-Muslim, and anti-immigrant policies? Will nativist movements continue to emerge, like they have throughout the larger history of this nation?

Using the case of Iranians in diaspora, this book has called attention to how modern Western democracies persistently use the language of liberalism and universalism while simultaneously practicing a politics of racial/ethnic exclusion. The lived experiences of Iranians uncover how "unconditional belonging" and access to the full benefits of social membership remain racialized and the ideal citizen continues to be white and Christian.

ACKNOWLEDGMENTS

Conditional Belonging has been over ten years in the making. Along this journey, I have been blessed with mentors who have guided me and helped me grow as a scholar. At the University of California, Davis, I was encouraged by Dina Okamoto to conduct an Honors Thesis Research paper on second-generation Iranians in northern California that ignited the larger intellectual curiosities that are detailed in this book. At Temple University, Rosario Espinal, Peter Gran, Sherri Grasmuck, and Mary Stricker were rigorous and passionate teachers and mentors. My dissertation chair and mentor Michelle Byng blessed me, inspired me, and helped me grow in ways she may never know. I am indebted to her for holding me to a high standard, for life lessons inside and outside of the academy, and for teaching me the importance of telling our stories. I am also grateful to Anthony Monteiro's semester-long course on the scholarship of W. E. B. Du Bois. The conversations in that class are still with me. I would not be where I am today without the good fortune of supportive teachers and mentors. Thank you for believing in me and guiding me.

I am forever indebted to the individuals who spent many hours talking with me and sharing intimate, and sometimes painful, aspects of their lives and experiences. Thank you for opening your homes to me, introducing me to your children, friends, and families, inviting me to events, feeding me, supporting me and this project, and trusting me with your stories. This book would have been impossible without you.

I am also grateful to the supportive community I found in Hamburg. Thank you for showing me around Hamburg, taking me along to events with you, and welcoming me into your spaces and communities. Thank you to Ludwig Paul at the University of Hamburg for your generosity while I was conducting fieldwork in Germany, and Ramin Shaghaghi for helping me get acquainted with Iranian associations and organizations. I am also appreciative of DIWAN, the Deutsch-Iranischer Akademiker Club of Hamburg, and the Deutsch-Iranische Gesellschaft of Hamburg.

The research presented in this book was supported in part by the Graduate School at Temple University, start-up research funds at Muhlenberg College, and support from the Faculty Summer Research Grant and Faculty Research and Professional Growth Grant. Thank you to my colleagues at Muhlenberg College, especially Janine Chi, Benjamin Carter, Irene Chien, Maura Finkelstein, Casey Miller, Robin Riley-Casey, Lora Taub, and the funding bodies, especially the FDSC, who have supported my work. A special shout-out to my undergraduate research assistants, Bridget Cantor, Alison Cummins, and Michelle Sanchez, for helping transcribe interviews. Thank you also to my incredible students, past and present, in the Sociology and Anthropology Department and larger Muhlenberg College campus who have been a source of inspiration and intellectual curiosity.

Many scholars and friends have influenced my scholarship, some providing generous thoughts and feedback on conference presentations, papers, and projects. Thank you to Beeta Baghoolizadeh, Narges Bajoghli, Yousef Baker, Mehdi Bozorgmehr, Louise Cainkar, Arlene Dallalfar, Arash Davari, Tanya Golash-Boza, Mary Hovsepian, Atiya Husain, Persis Karim, Neda Maghbouleh, Amy Malek, Mohsen Mobasher, and Hamid Naficy.

Audiences at the annual conferences of the American Sociological Association, Eastern Sociological Society, and Iranian Studies Association provided space and feedback while I worked through various sections of the data chapters. I am grateful to the editors, reviewers, and readers at New York University Press for helping this manuscript take shape. A special thank you to Ilene Kalish who, from our very first conversation, believed in this project. My endless appreciation to the two anonymous readers who showed great care and critical insight and took the time to help make this manuscript what it is now. Thank you to Trevor Perri for your encouragement, comments, and suggestions. This manuscript is better because of your careful reading and helpful feedback.

To my friends and chosen community, I want to acknowledge my Philly community, Corinne Castro, Nyron Crawford, Marco Hill, Diane Garbow, Shari Gilmore, Darryl Miller, Duiji Mshinda, Biany Perez, Laura Krystal Porterfield, Brittany Webb, and my sis-star circle, Shesheena Bray, Nuala Cabral, Christina Jackson, Nehad Khader, Koren Martin, Tarisse Iriarte-Medina, Mari Morales, Jackie Rios, Sheena Sood, and Anissa Weinraub—thank you for holding space for me, your beautiful energy, light, and all the love. Also, a special shout-out to the Lucky Goat coffee shop crew, especially Ms. Toyin, Amanda, Bamidele, and Paul. I also want to acknowledge my friends and colleagues in California, Dalita and Edward Lara, Daniel Olmos, Steven Osuna, and Cesar Rodriguez, and my dear friends Tiffany Berry, Amaka Okechukwu and Matt Birkhold for their care, support, and friendship over the years. I also want to acknowledge the "Lake Merritt Chill Association," aka Dana, David, and our most recent member, Baby Melo, for all the love, joy, and adventures.

To my family: thank you to Hossein Sadeghi, Abdol-Hossein Sadeghi, Batul Sadeghi, for praying for me, loving me, and believing in me. Thank you to my many cousins and family members living in Canada, Iran, and across Europe for their encouragement. I want to thank Nahid Davoudinejad for supporting and believing in me, inshallah one day we won't be separated by continents. I also want to thank Khazar Khakbaz for being the best cousin, and sister, I could have asked for. Ruhe Akram Sadeghi, Faranak Sadeghi, Ismael Kalantari, and Saeed Kalantari shad bashe—I know that you are watching me and that you are proud of me. Yek ruz hamdigaro baz dobare mibinim. Baba bozorg: "giiiii dusted daram!!" And finally, mamnoon to my Maman va Baba joon for all their sacrifices, for setting the bar high, for teaching me how to stand strong, for giving me the freedom to be me, for believing in me and my dreams, and for inspiring me to live with purpose. I am forever grateful. Lastly, thank you to God for guiding my path and bestowing mercy and grace. As my elders say, "dast be kar, del ba yar."

APPENDIX: RESEARCH METHODOLOGY

The research that informs this book is inductive and aimed at understanding how critical international events and global and state policy affect processes of racialization, politicization, and social membership. The data for this book draw on two qualitative methods: structured and open-ended interviews and participant observation. The use of qualitative inquiry is connected to the desire to understand the experiences of individuals from their perspective and standpoint.[1] Human lived experience is at the center of qualitative inquiry and can reveal, describe, and map the lived experiences of others.[2] In-depth interviewing helps us go beyond commonsense explanations for understanding a given phenomenon, activity, or practice and "explore the contextual boundaries of that experience or perception, to uncover what is usually hidden from ordinary view or reflection or to penetrate to more reflective understandings about the nature of that experience."[3]

I wanted to document how state policies enacted to combat terrorism, as well as mainstream suspicion and prejudice toward Middle Easterners and Muslims following September 11, 2001, were reflected in the lives of Iranians in diaspora.[4] Scholarship and theories on migration and race/ethnicity facilitated my interest in understanding how national and global context can mediate and influence how immigrants perceive and understand their place in their new nation. Specifically, a project detailing the lives of Iranian immigrants, whom some scholars[5] consider economically and professionally successful, could produce further knowledge about how immigrant groups whose homeland is politically stigmatized experience belonging and social citizenship comparatively. I was especially interested in understanding if and how national context with its respective racial and citizenship regime mediate and shape racialization, politicization, and social membership. Conducting in-depth interviews was one of the most effective ways through which I could understand and examine the lived experiences of Iranians in diaspora.

FIELDWORK

The larger project was carried out over a total of nine years, in two waves, and across three different regions. In total, I conducted 112 interviews with first-, 1.5-, and second-generation Iranians in three main regions of Iranian immigrant settlement: northern and southern California and Hamburg, Germany. The first wave of interviews consisted of eighty-eight interviews and formed the basis and foundation of my 2014 project, and my larger interests in detailing how global and national politics combined with systems of racial stratification impact belonging and racialization. The second wave started in the summer of 2016 and consisted of twenty-four follow-up interviews with Iranians whom I had spoken to five and six years prior. Out of this larger sample, the lived experiences of eighty-eight participants form the empirical basis for the data presented throughout the book.

The logic behind the need for follow-up research emerged in the fall of 2015 when the refugee crisis in Europe was underway. I was in the middle of my first year as visiting assistant professor at Muhlenberg College, and I felt compelled to conduct follow-up research because I was deeply mindful of how the acceptance of approximately 1.2 million new refugees would impact German society. In the summer of 2016, I returned to Hamburg and conducted follow-up interviews with a total of twelve first- and second-generation Iranians I had previously spoken with in 2011. These follow-up interviews form a portion of the data found in chapters 3 and 4, especially as it relates to racialization, racial boundaries, and belonging in Germany. I also conducted ethnographic research; I visited several refugee camps, spoke with Iranians who were participating in refugee resettlement initiatives and programs, visited Iranian businesses that I had previously patronized, and attended social and cultural events throughout Hamburg, as well as academic-centered ones sponsored through the University of Hamburg.

Similarly, with the election of Donald Trump, I was acutely aware that the lives of Iranians in the US would be impacted and changed dramatically, and this motivated the twelve follow-up interviews with Iranians in northern and southern California in the summer and fall of 2017 and 2018. The follow-up interviews were critical as they allowed me to detail how the changing social and political climate had impacted Iranians in real time. This further strengthened and solidified the findings in the initial research about the role of global politics in the racialization and politicization of Iranians found in the second and fourth chapters of the book. Finally, in the summer of 2019, I was in the final stages of research and returned to LA for further ethnographic research. I patronized Iranian businesses in the Westwood area of Los Angeles, a central part of "Tehrangeles," and had numerous (unrecorded) conversations with owners and managers, as well as patrons who would sometimes spontaneously join our conversations. This sort of active participant observation highlighted, once again, the diversity of experiences and opinion among the larger Iranian American community in the US, especially as it relates to global politics and the United States' relationship with Iran. Some of my observations about the support for the Trump administration among a portion of the first generation found in chapter 2 were informed by these conversations.

The longitudinal approach in qualitative research is challenging, as each subsequent sample will become smaller because of attrition. For example, some of the respondents had contact info that was no longer valid, some did not respond to requests for follow-up interviews, and others were unable to participate because of time and work constraints. Yet those that did participate in the follow-up interviews provided invaluable insight into how the racialization and politicization of Iranians is intimately connected to global and national events and dynamics. Given that we had a sense of familiarity with one another, and I knew aspects of their experiences from our previous conversation, I was able to explore certain topics further than in our first interview. In this sense, the follow-up interviews were richer in that I could explore certain topics and themes more deeply. The five-year gap between the first and second wave of research had also given me time to document the major social and political changes that had occurred and further analyze what the comparative case could tell us about processes of racialization, politicization, and belonging. The follow-up research allowed me to document how belonging and social membership shift and fluctuate according to social and political climate, how racial projects have ebbs and flows, and how the rise of anti-immigrant and anti-Muslim rhetoric and policy impact the daily lives of Iranians within and outside of Iran.

The sample was evenly divided by gender and generation, and most of the respondents in both the US and Germany were raised in secular Muslim households and continued to be secular. A few told me that they were practicing Muslims. The sample in the US also contained a few second-generation Armenian Iranians who had one Iranian and one Armenian parent. These individuals were also raised in secular households. The interviews were semi-structured and contained open-ended interview questions, so that participants did not feel constrained to respond in predetermined ways and could provide information that may not have been anticipated by me. The interviews with first-generation Iranians were mostly in Persian, unless they preferred to use English or German, and the second-generation interviews were mostly conducted in English. My interview questionnaire explored the following themes: belonging, inclusion/exclusion, experiences with discrimination and marginality, issues related to national, racial/ethnic, and religious identity, matters related to acquiring settlement resources, and citizenship. I asked about their migration stories, including the reasons why they migrated from Iran, why they chose the US or Germany as their nation of settlement, and what visions and expectations they had before migration, as well as their early migration experiences. These inquiries helped provide some context into why and under what circumstances

Iranians left Iran. It also allowed me to examine some of the differences between Iranians who migrated to the US and Germany, and how their experiences of migration and settlement may have influenced their feelings of belonging and membership. Specific questions were also asked about American and German national narratives, the main values and characteristics of these nations, and Iranians' perceptions of how immigrants are received and treated. I also inquired about whether the immigrants' nation of origin matters in how they are received in the US and Germany. These questions allowed me to analyze Iranians' perceptions of the American and German national contexts, the values they deemed important to attain employment and educational opportunities, the barriers to their success, the factors that facilitated their ability to belong, and the circumstances that led them to not experience belonging. I was also able to gauge whether they saw contradictions between America's and Germany's official declarations of how immigrants and racial/ethnic and religious minorities are received and treated, and Iranians' perceptions of immigrants' actual treatment. Iranians were also asked about what they enjoyed most about their lives in the US and Germany and the factors that made their lives difficult. This allowed me to gauge whether there were similar or overlapping factors that impacted the lives of Iranians.

Respondents were also asked about their experiences in education and schooling, the labor market, and the acquisition of resources for housing. These probes helped me to assess how experiences of acquiring resources in a variety of settings and institutions influenced their sense of belonging and membership. I also investigated the extent to which Iranians were affected by the perceptions that "others" had about their group and about the politics surrounding Iran, and how these perceptions affected their everyday lives. The combination of these inquiries helped me uncover the extent of Iranians' encounters with mainstream stereotypes about their racial/ethnic group and how they utilize public dialogue about Iranians and Middle Easterners, Iran, and the region of the Middle East in their narrations of belonging.

In both the US and Germany, my professional, friendship, and familial networks played a significant role in helping me find research respondents by circulating my call for participants and introducing me to a variety of Iranian academic, cultural, and professional associations and organizations in the Bay Area, southern California, and Hamburg. Most of the Iranians I spoke with in both nations were recruited through snowball sampling. I also spent a considerable amount of time patronizing Iranian businesses and attending social and community events hosted by various Iranian community associations and organizations in northern and southern California and Hamburg. I observed Iranians in many different spaces, including social and cultural events, political gatherings, and religious ones. Iranian student groups at multiple universities were also instrumental as they allowed me to introduce my project at their events and widely posted my call for research participants. I also audited Persian-language courses and seminars in Iranian studies programs. Through my relationships with the faculty and students, I was invited to numerous cultural and social events attended by many in the Iranian community. Throughout this project, close attention was paid to protecting sensitive information about the participants' identities and maintaining the anonymity of the respondents; pseudonyms are used for all but two of the interlocutors.

LIMITATIONS AND OTHER OBSERVATIONS

A methodological concern I had at the beginning of this research was my position as an "insider." As a child of Iranian immigrants who had been born in Iran and raised in both the US and Germany, I had invaluable insight into what living in each nation felt like. I also spoke English and Persian fluently, and after a few weeks in Germany, my German was also almost fluent again. I was aware of the benefits my position held, but also knew that this status came with responsibility. As an "insider," I knew I would have easier access to the Iranian community, that they would be more willing to share their stories with me, and that they would see me as one of them. In prior decades, social researchers, especially those that stress positivism and purported that research could be "objective," frowned upon a humanistic and interpretive-centered approach to research. In recent years, more and more sociologists, especially feminist scholars, have stressed that lived experience is not only an asset but an important source of knowledge production and epistemology, especially for those whose stories have so often been marginalized and left out of scholarly research and theory.[6] In this regard, I am conscious to not assume or take anything for granted during the research process, with the awareness that my "insider status," proximity to the research, and lived experiences as an Iranian immigrant have been invaluable to my "hunches," insights, theoretical lenses, and how this project was ultimately carried out.

Given that this is a formative study of the Iranian community in the US, there are a few limitations. One is that the US sample is solely derived from the state of California. Although there were methodological justifications for keeping the US sample to California, I recognize that the racial/ethnic and economic characteristics of Midwestern, Southern, or East Coast states could produce differing experiences for Iranians. It is possible that sampling Iranians in the Midwest, South, and the Northeast would bring forth varying narratives of belonging[7] and processes of racialization. Future research on Iranians living in different regions of the US may potentially be able to speak to this.

There were also some noteworthy observations that emerged in the fieldwork. For example, the Iranians that I encountered in the US, specifically the first generation, were guarded and some expressed concern about being interviewed. There were questions about the interviews being recorded and where the data would end up; others wanted to know my personal history and the history of my parents' migration before they felt comfortable talking to me. Although all these individuals were in the US legally and most were citizens, they felt uneasy around certain themes. I believe that this general sentiment of uneasiness and doubt among the first generation in the US is undoubtedly linked to their fears of being surveilled or targeted by the American government because of their Iranian identity. This was especially evident among those who had migrated during, or lived through, the hostage crisis and had experienced difficulties. Interestingly, this sentiment was virtually absent in Germany, even though a good portion of the first-generation sample in Germany had been politically active in Iran and attained residency in Germany through political asylum. They did not seem to have apprehensions or worries about being interviewed for this research, even though some of their migration stories tended to be more complicated and even traumatic. Most of the Iranians sampled in the US were not politically active in Iran and did not come from political families— thus their anxieties struck me as interesting. It is possible that Iranians in Germany feel safer and more protected by the German state than those living in the US. These differences may also speak to how global politics surrounding Iran, and the larger Middle East, may cause Iranians in the US to have more anxiety surrounding issues concerning Iran compared to those living in Germany, specifically because of the history of deportation of Iranians during the hostage crisis years, as well as surveillance after 9/11. All in all, these observations were noteworthy and eye-catching.

Lastly, I also made some interesting observations about the generational differences among the Iranians that participated in this research. Follow-up interviews with second-generation Iranian Americans, in particular, revealed a heightened sense of social and political awareness and consciousness. When the 1.5- and second-generation Iranians were initially interviewed for this project, they were mostly young adults, college aged. During the first wave of interviews, there was a sense of profound hope that, with the election of Barack Obama, the Bush era was "behind us" and that America was on the path toward progress. Characterizations of America as exemplifying a "color-blind" or "post-racial" ethos were prominent throughout the interviews. Following the election of Donald Trump, and the rise of far-right ideology and explicit forms of racism, Iranians experienced a shift in thinking and expressed a sense that the US was "perhaps moving backward socially and politically." While the impact of social movements and geopolitics on political consciousness is not within the scope of this research, I do believe that broader social and political movements such as Black Lives Matter and #MeToo, continued military occupation in the Middle East, the two-decade-long war in Afghanistan, and the global pandemic, along with the ever-rising economic inequalities in the US, are influencing the second generation. Future research on second-generation Iranians in diaspora will hopefully examine the role of national and global politics and social movements on political socialization and mobilization.

NOTES

INTRODUCTION

1 By 1999 the children and grandchildren of the initial guest workers had lived their entire lives in Germany but were not citizens and did not possess political and civil rights (Joppke 1999). This population was a key motivation for the changes to the citizenship law.

2 Alba 2005.

3 Vasquez (2010) defines flexible ethnicity as "the ability to deftly and effectively navigate different racial terrains and be considered an 'insider' in more than one racial or ethnic group" (p. 46).

4 Three recent full-length books about Iranians are Mohsen Mobasher's *Iranians in Texas* (2012), which explores ethnic identity and political nature of Iranians' migration and integration into the US; Neda Maghbouleh's *The Limits of Whiteness: Iranians and the Everyday Politics of Race* (2017), a seminal study of the Iranian American community that significantly contributes to the scarce but emerging research on Iranians and race; and *The Iranian Diaspora: Challenges, Negotiations, and Transformations* (2018), a collection edited by Mobasher of recent research on Iranians globally that outlines the differences and similarities in experiences of integration since the revolution.

5 See, e.g., Thomson and Crul 2007; Haasler 2020.

6 Ansari 1977; Bakalian and Bozorgmehr 2005; Bozorgmehr 2000; Chaichain 1997; Daha 2011; Dallalfar 1994; Darvishpour 2002; Der-Martirosian 2008; Ghorashi 1997; Hosseini-Kaladjahi 1997; Khosravi 1999; Lewin 2002; Lindert et al. 2008; Maghbouleh 2017; Mahdavi 2006; Malek 2019; Marvasti and McKinney 2004; McAuliffe 2007; Min and Bozorgmehr 2000; Moallem 2003; Mobasher 2012; Mostofi 2003; Sadeghi 2016, 2018a; Safi 2010; Tehranian 2009.

7 Benedict Anderson (1983) coined the concept of an "imagined community" as a way to describe how nation-states are socially constructed communities by those who perceive themselves as part of that group. According to Arnold, imagined communities are "to be distinguished, not by their falsity/genuineness, but by the style in which they are imagined" (p. 6).

8 Fredrickson 2002; Anderson 1983.

9 Bruner 2011; Muller 2006.

10 Mills 1997.

11 Fredrickson 2002.

12 Aleinikoff and Rumbaut 1998; Behdad 2005.

13 Steinberg 2001.

14 Kerber 1997, 843.

15 Tehranian 2008.

16 Cainkar 2006; Gualtieri 2009; Tehranian 2008.

17 Overwhelmingly, the early twentieth-century waves of Arab immigrants to the US were of Christian faith, which significantly helped their placement in the white racial category (Cainkar 2006; Tehranian 2008).

18 Immigrants from the southern and eastern parts of the world, especially Africa, Asia, South America, and the West Indies, did not immigrate in significant numbers until 1965.

19 Bonilla-Silva 2017.

20 Bonilla-Silva 1997.

21 Bonilla-Silva 2017.

22 Bonilla-Silva 2004.

23 Ozkirimli 2010, 15.

24 The work of Brubaker (1992), Gilroy (1992), Giroux (1995), Bonilla-Silva (2000), Green (2000), Alba (2005o, and Muller (2011) have addressed the importance of ethno-cultural nationalism in the construction of the German state, and its national identity. Blood-based conceptions of citizenship and belonging were crucial in the formation of the *Volk*, the German people. These conceptions continue to influence Germany's national narrative, its national identity, and its ideal imaged community.

25 Bonilla-Silva 2000; El-Tayeb 1999; Mueller 2011.

26 Anderson 1983; El-Tayeb 1999; Brubaker 1992.

27 Brubaker 1992, 188.

28 Mueller 2012.

29 Fredrickson 2002.

30 Fredrickson (2002) describes how the Hitler regime saw Jews as evil in spirit and body; this was more than biological racism, but a kind of racism that was mixed with mythology and ideas of evil. Jews were constructed as "devious and cunning" and liable to "pollute and seduce Germans."

31 Gesley 2017.

32 The Basic Law for the Federal Republic of Germany is the constitution of the Federal Republic of Germany. Article 16a specifically declares the right to asylum, stating that "persons persecuted on political grounds shall have the right of asylum" (https://perma.cc/RW2X-HD46).

33 Article 1a(2) of the Refugee Convention states that a refugee is someone who, "owing to a well-founded fear of being persecuted for reasons of race, religion, nationality, membership of a particular social group or political opinion, is outside the country of his nationality, and is unable to, or owing to such fear, is unwilling to avail himself of the protection of that country" (www.gesetze-im-internet.de/asylvfg_1992/index.html).

34 Bonilla-Silva 2000; Carrera 2006.
35 El-Tayeb 1999; Mueller 2012; Weber 2016.
36 Mueller 2012; Silverstein 2005.
37 Bonilla-Silva and Mayorga 2011, 2.
38 Omi and Winant 1986; Barot and Bird 2001.
39 Said 1978; Amanat 2011.
40 Goldberg 2008, 163.
41 Gotanda 2011.
42 Miller 2003; Levitt and Schiller 2004.
43 Shotter 1993.
44 Glenn 2002, 196.

CHAPTER 1. LAYERED AND COMPLICATED

1 Hakimzadeh 2006.
2 Hamid Dabashi (2007) argues that the cause of the coup was rooted in the conflict between Russia and the British and was orchestrated by them.
3 Zimmerman 2018.
4 Khatib-Shahidi 2013.
5 Germany also supplied sixty-five locomotives for the 1938 opening. The main train station in Tehran was built by Frankfurt-based Phillipp Holzmann AG.
6 Siemens has been doing business in Iran for over 150 years (Khatib-Shahidi 2013).
7 Clarkson 2013.
8 Khatib-Shahidi 2013.
9 Chehabi 2012.
10 Ibid.
11 Clarkson 2013.
12 Dabashi (2007) has argued that, for the upper-class members of Iranian society, the attainment of educational training in the US and Europe was a way to facilitate economic relations and further their personal interests.
13 Destatis 2011.
14 Dabashi 2007.
15 Tarock 1996.
16 British Petroleum was founded in 1939 as the Anglo-Persian Oil Company and had for decades exploited Iranian oil (Dabashi 2007).
17 The Consortium Agreement of 1954 provided Western oil companies with 40 percent of Iranian oil production.
18 Fatemi 1980, 308.
19 Prior to the revolution, Bank of America, Chase Manhattan Bank, Citibank, and Continental Illinois Bank of Chicago all generated income through interest, banking services, and returns on their foreign investments (Fatemi 1980).
20 Ibid.

21 Shannon 2015; Menashri 1992.

22 US Department of Homeland Security, Statistical Yearbook.

23 Hakimzadeh 2006.

24 Davar 2020.

25 In a Migration Policy Institute report by Hakimzadeh (2006), it was estimated that "in the 1977–1978 academic year, about 100,000 Iranians were studying abroad, of whom 36,220 were enrolled in U.S. institutes of higher learning; the rest were mainly in the United Kingdom, West Germany, France, Austria, and Italy." The report further estimates that by the following academic year that figure increased to 45,340 and peaked at 51,310 in 1979–1980.

26 Bozorgmehr and Sabbagh 1988.

27 Bozorgmehr (1998) cites data stating that by the mid-1970s approximately half of the student population that was abroad was in the US. Furthermore, the migratory circumstances and patterns of pre-revolution student migrants to Western nations were intended to be temporary, yet the Iranian Revolution made their migration permanent.

28 Bozorgmehr 1998; Hakimzadeh 2006.

29 Given the scarcity of research on Iranians in the social science scholarship, it is difficult to locate literature that addresses these organizations, which specialized in sending Iranians abroad for education. However, follow-up conversations with my respondents confirmed that the Edaraye Pasireshe Daneshju was an organization in Iran that specialized in preparing required college materials for Iranians wanting to go to Western educational institutions.

30 Both of my interviews with him, the initial and follow-up, were conducted in this office.

31 After our interview, he gave me an extensive tour of his research facilities at the University of Hamburg. He also shared details about his yearly international research trips and the training of PhD students. His expertise is rare, and I better understood why he was recruited to come to Germany.

32 Malvern, Arkansas, as mentioned by Houshang, was home to Reynolds Metal Company. It was one of the main aluminum production plants in Arkansas before closing in 1985.

33 For the past thirty years, Kimia has gone to the US at least once or twice a year to visit her family, and she spoke to me in detail about the differences she had observed between the nations.

34 This disparity is reflected in my sample; there were only three single women in the sample compared to nine single men.

35 According to Tarock (1996), with the growing strength of Islamist movements in Sudan, Egypt, Algeria, Malaysia, and Indonesia, the Iranian Revolution had deep geopolitical implications for the US. It signaled a challenge to "western social and political domination of the third world" (p. 163).

36 Naficy 2012.

37 I remember seeing this movie at the theater with my mom and her German friend when I was a kid in Germany. I was unable to express why the movie made me uncomfortable at the time, but it was terrible, and I remember feeling terrible. The way they showed Iranian families, our food, and culture felt strange to me. I have faint memories of my mom and her friend discussing the movie afterward, and my mom seemed irritated and offended.

38 Naficy 2012.

39 There was an exponential increase in news coverage of Iran: from 9.8 minutes in 1977 to 381.7 minutes in 1979 and 368.9 minutes in 1980 (Naficy 2012).

40 Mahdavi (2006) highlights how growing anti-Iranian prejudice in the US during the revolution and hostage crisis made Iranians targets of discrimination.

41 Tehranian 2009.

42 According to Bozorgmehr (2007), the "Iranian Control Program" screened approximately fifty-seven thousand Iranian students to verify that they had legal status. Furthermore, each student had to register with the INS by mid-December 1979, have a valid visa, and provide proof of full-time school enrollment. Those who failed to comply with the INS were at risk for deportation.

43 The *Washington Post* reported on December 28, 1979, that the US Court of Appeals approved Iranian student deportations. On November 13, 1979, Iranian students in the US had been asked to register with an INS office or risk being deported.

44 Said 1978; Amanat 2011.

45 Akram and Johnson 2002; Tehranian 2009.

46 According to their mission statement, the International Rescue Committee "responds to the world's worst humanitarian crises and helps people to survive and rebuild their lives. The IRC offers lifesaving care and life-changing assistance to refugees forced to flee from war or disaster."

47 The latter of which was eliminated under the Trump presidency.

48 Bozorgmehr (1998) and Hakimzadeh (2006) describe the ways in which Iranians came to the US after the revolution. This process commonly entailed Iranians coming to the US through a third country and filing for asylum after arriving.

49 Hakimzadeh 2006.

50 Destatis 2011.

51 Clayton and Holland 2015.

52 UNHCR 2020.

53 OECD 2013.

54 Degler and Liebig 2017.

55 This shows up again in the follow-up interviews in 2016, when an Iranian explained to me how Iranians are not truly *badbakht* (ill-fated, or victims of unfortunate circumstance), but rather lack social and political freedom, and economic opportunities, in Iran.

56 Portes and Manning (1986) have shown that Cuban immigrants from earlier waves of migration, which were primarily made up of the elite and professional classes, overwhelmingly opposed to Fidel Castro's government, and sympathetic to the US were considered political refugees and received tremendous federal assistance, which helped them comfortably settle in the US. The Mariel refugees who came in the early 1980s were mostly ineligible for financial and relocation support because they were defined as economic migrants (Zucker 1983; Portes and Manning 1986).

57 Mitchell 1989; Portes and Manning 1986; Zucker 1983.

58 See Crul and Doomernik 2003; Crul and Schneider 2009; Crul and Vermeulen 2003.

59 The focus on educational and economic institutions and institutional arrangements helps us see, for example, why and how second-generation Turks across several European countries fared better educationally than they did in Germany (Crul and Schneider 2009).

CHAPTER 2. GUILTY BY ASSOCIATION

1 Hamid Naficy has shown the negative cultural imagery of Iran and Iranians in the US during the hostage crisis.

2 The term "foreign terrorists" illustrates the administration's view of Iranian nationals and others from Muslim-majority nations.

3 The Center for Constitutional Rights (2019) highlighted how the travel ban caused Iranians and other nations from targeted countries to lose access to immigrant and diversity visas. The visas available to them were F, M, and J visas, whose applicants are subjected to enhanced screenings and requirements.

4 Khaled 2020.

5 After decades of strife between the US and Iran, the Iran Deal was supposed to become one of the Obama administration's greatest achievements.

6 This hope was especially pronounced among Iranians in Iran and those in diaspora, as they hoped that diplomacy would finally bring the two nations together after thirty-nine years.

7 This does not deviate from George W. Bush's speech at the United Nations General Assembly on January 29, 2002, when he stated that Iran, along with Iraq and North Korea, was a part of the "Axis of Evil."

8 Bajoghli 2019.

9 Chappell 2019.

10 Parsi 2019.

11 This include a more recent incident in the Persian Gulf region in which Iranian Revolutionary Guards shot down an unmanned drone that they claimed was flying in Iranian airspace and collecting intelligence information. The US military and Trump administration denied this and claimed that the drone was flying in international airspace. Several days later, it was reported that the US was primed

to retaliate with a jet attack, but this was decided against in the last minutes because Trump felt that killing scores of people "would not be 'proportionate to shooting down an unmanned drone'" (Shear, Cooper, and Schmitt 2019).

12 Messner 2012.

13 Maghbouleh 2017.

14 Naficy 2012.

15 It is this same rhetoric and consequent policy of the Bush administration that led the US to start wars in Iraq and Afghanistan; continue its presence in the Middle East, which now also includes Syria and Yemen; and back additional proxy wars.

16 Cainkar 2009; Tehranian 2009.

17 US Department of State 2017.

18 BBC News 2010.

19 NIAC 2010.

20 The Iranian community in the US is quite diverse, politically, religiously, economically, and racially/ethnically. There are those in the Iranian community, especially those in southern California, who are self-declared "royalists" and maintain support for the return of a monarchy in Iran. These Iranian Americans tend to be wealthier, and have more conservative views about immigration, the economy, and foreign policy in the Middle East.

21 I have now visited Iran three times since I was a young child, and some family members in diaspora have made similar remarks about safety and the "possibility of being arrested."

22 O'Connor 2018.

23 A December 2019 BBC report highlights five major ways that sanctions have hit Iran: massive recession, devaluation of the rial, the plummeting of oil exports, rising cost of living, and increasing gas prices.

24 Setayesh and Mackey 2016.

25 The high concentration of well-to-do and wealthier Iranians is well noted in the research on the Iranian American immigrants and ethnic entrepreneurs.

26 Numerous articles decsrbive the ways in which Iranians have been most affected by the Muslim Ban. Some scholars have argued that the Muslim Ban is in some ways more accurately depicted as an "Iran Ban," given that Iranian nationals tend to apply for and receive the highest number of student and travel visas among the sanctioned countries (Rezaian 2018; Gladstone 2018).

27 There are Iranian American individuals and families who are suing the Trump administration on the grounds of illegal detainment, harassment, and the separation of families (Sanchez 2019).

28 Malek 2019.

29 In some ways, Tony's worries have been substantiated. The US decision to leave the Iran Deal has had severe consequences for European nations

wanting economic relations with Iran; many countries have had to place business contracts on hold or even terminate them in response to US political pressure. Iranians who hold EU citizenship are also now required to apply for a visa to visit the US, meaning that they are no longer able to take advantage of the Visa Waiver Program (US Department of State, Visa Waiver Program, https://travel.state.gov/content/travel/en/us-visas/tourism-visit/visa-waiver-program.html). For instance, a news article from May 7, 2019, reported how an Iranian German father holding EU citizenship was denied a visa to come to his son's funeral in the US (Wright 2019).

30 Nick stated that he watched an interaction between a younger white woman and two elderly Asian women. While he did not intervene, he did speak to the elderly women after and told them, "They had a right to speak whatever language they wished, and not to listen to that woman."

31 It should be noted that, throughout my interviews in both nations, Iranians repeatedly respond to experiences of prejudice and racism by stating, "these people are uneducated," "they don't even read," or that they "lack culture." White Americans, especially, are regarded as being "cowboys."

32 An anecdote about my own seventh-grade yearbook in 1993—with regard to the racist things written in it—started an entire conversation about Nader's yearbook that he had recently found.

33 Bayoumi 2009; Cainkar 2009; Maira 2009; Selod 2015; Tehranian 2009.

CHAPTER 3. REFUGEES AND *AUSLÄNDERS*

1 Aleinikoff and Klusmeyer 2000.

2 Oezcan 2004.

3 Goldberg 2008.

4 Goldberg (2008) argues that the rising population of Muslims in Europe has led to rising narratives of Muslims culturally "polluting" Europe.

5 Fredrickson 2002.

6 Alternative for Germany (AfD) is a right-wing political party that promotes traditional Christian values, is skeptical of the EU and climate change, and is against immigration.

7 This became especially apparent during the 2015 refugee crisis, when Germany was the sole country that accepted refugees without condition, unlike Italy, Greece, France, the UK, and many others.

8 These data themes and findings emerged when I asked specific questions about German citizenship and equality, not questions about belonging and social membership.

9 According to Destatis (2015), "the migration status of a person is determined based on his/her own characteristics immigration, naturalisation and citizenship and the relevant characteristics of his/her parents."

10 The literal meaning of this term is someone from "outside the land."

11 Boundary-making theories have been employed to highlight the boundary negotiations and incorporation patterns of immigrants and their children outside of the US context (Alba 2005; Zolberg and Woon 1999), identify the role of institutions and socio-cultural and legal domains in shaping the "immigrant-native boundary" (Alba 2005; Bonilla-Silva 2000), examine the role of culture, institutions, and social networks in the production of ethnic, symbolic and social boundaries and forms of belonging (Lamont and Molinar 2002; Wimmer 2013), and identify the social processes that produce inequality, stigmatization, and racialization (Lamont, Beljean, and Clair 2014).

12 My experiences in grade school in Germany as well as high school in the US attest to the important role that interracial/interethnic friendship play in one feeling less marginalized and targeted in school. These friendship circles created a sense of comfort, common understanding, normalcy, and social bonds—a sense of someone "having your back."

13 Selod (2015) examines the gendered aspects of this racialization in her work on Muslim American men and women in the US. Specifically, Muslim women who veil are perceived as being disloyal to national values, while Muslim men were frequently criminalized for being Muslim, seen as being disloyal, and associated with terrorism.

14 The racialization of Islam and Muslims is rooted in the essentialization of race and cultural traits and practices. When Muslims are racialized, they are assumed to act in set ways, such as being very traditional, backward, not modern, uncivilized, and against Western culture. Racialization occurs when Muslims are seen as a monolithic group of people with certain stereotypical behaviors and attributes.

15 Said 1978.

16 Changing the ancestry criteria was a long battle; it was a combination of domestic and international factors that led to changes in Germany's citizenship policy. This included the seeming contradiction of granting automatic citizenship to those with German ancestry—many of whom who had not lived in Germany—while denying these rights to several generations of foreigners who had been born and raised in Germany. The SPD-led government officially removed descent-based criteria from German citizenship law, allowing foreigners to finally be able to naturalize.

17 Bonilla-Silva and Mayorga 2011.

18 Mills 1997.

19 The research of Worbs (2003) illustrates that second-generation immigrants in Germany also face structural challenges in education and the labor market. This is largely attributed to a German educational system that does not foster the academic advancement of children from underprivileged families, the high importance that is placed upon educational qualifications for attaining vocational training and access to the labor market, acts of discrimination, and the parental

generations' lack of social and cultural capital. Similarly, Crul and Doomernik (2003) found that, compared to their Dutch peers, Moroccan and Turks suffer from higher levels of unemployment and discrimination in labor market.

20 In the interview, Siavash mentioned how he had heard of foreigners whose asylum or residency cases were rejected or jeopardized in retaliation for their complaints about discriminatory treatment.

21 Deutsche Welle 2016; Weichselbaumer 2019.

22 Existing research on the Iranian diaspora in Europe has shown some general trends. For example, research in Sweden shows that Iranians' ability to partake in the formal labor market has been impeded by discrimination. Hosseini-Kaladjahi's (1997) study highlighted the fact that, despite Iranians' high levels of educational attainment, discriminatory practices and racial prejudice hindered their ability to achieve upward mobility in the labor market, and socially and culturally integrate into Sweden. Khosravi (1999) found that Iranians' aspirations to be self-employed were related to the high rates of unemployment among foreigners and their marginal position as result of being discriminated against in Swedish society.

23 Scholars such as Park and Burgess (1921) theorized that through the process of assimilation immigrants would be "incorporated in a common cultural life" (p. 735). They assumed that the assimilation process for immigrants was inevitable, progressing across generations until everyone was absorbed into the dominant culture. Gordon (1964) modified Park and Burgess's framework by arguing that the assimilation process would first involve immigrants losing their ethnic ties and heritages, which would give them the ability to move up the educational and occupational mobility ladder. His approach assumed that cultural assimilation would create a pathway toward structural assimilation.

24 UNHCR 2020.

25 Clayton and Holland 2015; Ostrand 2015.

26 Clayton and Holland 2015.

27 Ostrand 2015; Clayton and Holland 2015.

28 Deutsche Welle 2019.

29 Ibid.; BBC News 2019a.

30 Interestingly, this is similar to Iranians' responses to the election of Donald Trump in the US follow-up interviews in 2017–2018. Many I followed up with expressed surprise that America "was actually so racist."

31 The research by Beverly Weber (2016) shows how German media and social media accounts responded to the Cologne events, specifically, the racist discourses.

32 This was quite different than the climate evoked by Chancellor Angela Merkel's declaration on August 31, 2015, in a press conference at a refugee camp, that "wir schaffen das" ("we can do it" or "we will manage it"), in reference to taking in and "integrating" refugees (Delcker 2016).

33 Thomson and Crul 2007; Crul and Schneider 2009.

CHAPTER 4. RACIAL AND CULTURAL FLEXIBILITY

1 Bonilla-Silva (1997) defines racial structures as the social, political, and ideological practices that produce differential status between races. This includes laws regarding race, citizenship, amendments, constitution, enslavement based on color and descent, miscegenation laws, etc. These laws and policies have established different statuses and rights based on race.

2 Mostofi's (2003) research highlights that Iranians, like past immigrants, believe that being perceived as white and American, which includes the incorporation of American ideological norms, produces privilege in the US. Iranians utilize "whitening" strategies to blend into mainstream American society. She found that for Iranian Americans "the whiter the body, the more attractive the appearance, the greater the ability for assimilation of the public face, which translates to success" (p. 694).

3 Parvini and Ellis 2019.

4 Waters 1990.

5 Maghbouleh 2017.

6 Omi and Winant 1987.

7 I think these perceptions are deeply shaped by the presentation that Iranians themselves uphold. They also see themselves as being different from Arabs, Afghanis, Indians, etc.

8 Vasquez argues that "flexible ethnicity" is about being able to "effectively navigate different racial terrains and be considered 'an insider' in more than racial or ethnic group" (p. 46). It is also predicated upon being "whitened" or being racialized as non-Hispanic white. Flexible ethnicity underscores that racialization occurs on a continuum. The scholarship of Davila (2008), Golash-Boza and Darity (2008), and Vasquez (2010) all highlight the "racialization process continuum" in which "Latinos are simultaneously subjected to processes of whitening and racialization" (p. 12).

9 In the early part of the twentieth century, Italian Americans were not yet seen as white, but as "in-between" people and sometimes also as "race invaders" in the US. In Europe, those in the North consider Italians to be a part of the lower races of Europe (Richards 1999).

10 Blake 2010. Two aims of the campaign were to get a more accurate count of Iranians in the US and to create a MENA (Middle Eastern and North African) racial category in the 2020 census.

11 Waters 1990.

12 Davila 2008, 12.

13 Golash-Boza and Darity 2008; Vasquez 2010.

14 Selod 2015.

15 Glenn (2002) identifies three main components of social citizenship as *nationality* (being identified as a member of a particular nation), *standing* (being seen as a

capable and responsible member of society), and *allegiance* (being seen as a loyal member of the nation).

16 Sadeghi 2016; Sadeghi 2018a.

17 In my work, I have found that second-generation Iranians have significantly been steered away from religion in general, and also discouraged from political engagement, especially related to Iran. The desire to avoid political engagement is more profound among Iranians in the US. The work of Daha (2011) and Maghbouleh (2017) is important here as it relates to my discussion of how this concealment of identity is tied to racial trauma and the impact it has on the second generation. Daha's study of Iranian American adolescents illustrated that Iranian ethnic identity and loyalty was developed and reinforced through taking pride in Persian civilization and history, not being ashamed of having Iranian or Middle Eastern phenotypic features, resisting stereotypes about Iranian culture, and engaging with the Iranian community. Maghbouleh (2017) stresses the importance of "ethno-racial socialization" (p. 136), specifically the teaching of frameworks of political solidarity that help second-generation Iranians see and practice race as a political identity and work through past racial trauma.

18 Some of the experiences of my interlocutors are also reflected in scholarship on gender and integration among Iranians in Europe that has shown that Iranian women have been able to acculturate better and described more positive experiences than Iranian men (Lindert et al. 2008).

19 The idea that Iranian and other Middle Eastern women are "exotic" and thus attractive to Westerners, especially white men, is pronounced in both Germany and the US. In some instances, Iranian women believe this to be a compliment, something that works in their favor, while others find it offensive.

20 Some Iranian women did openly admit that dating foreign men, including Iranian men, would not benefit them in life or in securing a satisfactory quality of life. Some even made comments along the lines of "Now both of us will lose in the labor market; it's a double hit being coupled with a foreign man." These responses should be read as potential coping mechanisms to deal with the persistent anti-foreigner prejudice and structural racism in Germany.

21 In her follow-up interview in the summer of 2016, she told me that she was engaged to a German man and was getting ready to be married in the following months.

22 Interestingly, the Iranian men I spoke with who had German female partners did not necessarily see their lives improving in the same ways as Iranian women who had German male partners.

23 Vasquez 2010.

24 This is somewhat different than the narratives that I encountered from Iranians in the US about integration and their networks.

25 This "proving" (*Beweisen*) means that more effort is placed into explaining where one is "originally" from, what one is doing in Germany, and what one is

doing with their time here: Ultimately, are you being a good foreigner or bad one?

26 My conversations with Isabel brought up several memories of encounters I had as a child regarding Germany and dogs. A close friend of mine in grade school had a small dog, which we played with when I went over. While I was not allowed to have a dog or cat, I was not afraid of them. My mother on the other hand was uncomfortable and always acted very scared and jumpy when she came to pick me up from my friend's house. This embarrassed me because I felt that my mom should just "act normal around dogs and pet them." She always said it was because she didn't grow up with animals in the house in Iran, so she feared that they would bite her. Looking back, my friend's parents found this ridiculous at some point, I suppose, because they often rolled their eyes at my mom and made fun of her fear, like, "It's only a small dog, what's the big deal? Are you still scared of it?"

27 Whether it be the burden of the geopolitical relationship between the US and Iran, visibly practicing Islam, "looking brown, Arab, or Muslim," or being culturally "unintegrated."

28 Golash-Boza and Darity 2008; Vasquez 2010.

29 Maghbouleh (2017) highlights how Iranians and other SWANA populations, although legally classified as racially "white," do not reap the social benefits of the designation.

CONCLUSION

1 Ross 2021; Hussain 2021.

2 Paone and Thomas 2021.

3 DeYoung 2022.

4 DeLuce 2022.

5 These are slogans from AfD political campaigns and posters.

6 "Reclaim America" is a slogan of the US-based white supremacist group the Patriot Front (Syed 2019).

7 "The Reconquest" refers to "the historical period when Christians forces battled Muslims from the Iberian Peninsula" (Noack and Pannett 2021).

APPENDIX

1 Standpoint theory is rooted in the scholarship of Du Bois, especially his book *Dusk of Dawn* (1940), as well as the extensive work of Black feminist scholars (e.g., Davis 1981; hooks 1981; Collins 1999). This framework stresses the importance of lived experience and everyday experiences in the production of epistemology, especially suppressed and subjugated knowledge. Standpoint theory has been the foundation for Black feminist thought, activism, and scholarship, including theories of intersectionality.

2 Denzin 1991; Gubrium and Holstein 1997.

3 Johnson 2001, 106.

4 Scholars such as Bakalian and Bozorgmehr (2005), Byng (2008), Mahdavi (2006), Marvasti and McKinney (2004), and Tehranian (2009) have documented the racial profiling and discrimination that individuals of Middle Eastern background and those of the Muslim faith have faced as a result of the events that followed September 11, 2001.

5 Studies by Bozorgmehr (2007), Der-Martirosian (2008), Min and Bozorgmehr (2000), and Mostashari and Khodamhosseini (2004) have all shown that first-generation Iranian immigrants are among the most highly educated, high human-capital immigrant groups in the US.

6 See Alway 1995; Harding 2004; Collins 1999.

7 The multicultural characteristics of California and its reputation of "liberal" political policies may produce different perceptions of belonging than places where Iranians feel more racially/ethnically and culturally isolated, and where the political landscape is more conservative. It is also possible that Iranians' experiences of being able to be "honorary whites" is harder to approximate in places where there is a more explicit Black-white racial boundary.

BIBLIOGRAPHY

Akram, Susan M., and Kevin R. Johnson. 2002. "Race, Civil Rights, and Immigration Rights after September 11, 2001: The Targeting of Arabs and Muslims after 9/11." *NYU Annual Survey of American Law* 13 (36): 295–355.

Alba, Richard. 2005. "Bright vs. Blurred Boundaries: Second-Generation Assimilation and Exclusion in France, Germany, and the United States." *Ethnic and Racial Studies* 28: 20–49.

Alba, Richard, and Victor Nee. 2003. *Remaking the American Mainstream: Assimilation and Contemporary Immigration*. Cambridge, MA: Harvard University Press.

Aleinikoff, T. Alexander, and Doug B. Klusmeyer. 2000. *From Migrants to Citizens: Membership in a Changing World*. Washington, DC: Brookings Institution Press.

Aleinikoff, T. Alexander, and Rubén G. Rumbaut. 1998. "'Terms of Belonging: Are Models of Membership Self-Fulfilling Prophecies?" *Georgetown Immigration Law Journal* 13 (1): 1–24.

Alway, Joan. 1995. *Critical Theory and Political Possibilities*. Westport, CT: Greenwood Publishing.

Amanat, Abbas. 2011. "Introduction: Problematizing a Virtual Space." In *Is There a Middle East? The Evolution of a Geopolitical Concept*, edited by Michael E. Bonine, Abbas Amanat, and Michael Ezekiel Gasper. Palo Alto, CA: Stanford University Press.

American Civil Liberties Union. 2004. "Sanctioned Bias: Racial Profiling since 9/11." www.aclu.org.

Anderson, Benedict. 1983. *Imagined Communities: Reflections on the Origins and Spread of Nationalism*. New York: Verso.

Ansari, Abdolmaboud. 1977. "A Community in Process: The First Generation of the Iranian Professional Middle-Class Immigrants in the U.S." *International Review of Modern Sociology* 7 (June–July): 85–101.

———. 1988. *Iranian Immigrants in the United States: A Case Study of Dual Marginality*. New York: Associated Faculty Press.

Anvil, Merih. 2005. "No More Foreigners? The Remaking of German Naturalization and Citizenship Law, 1990 2000." *Dialectical Anthropology* 29: 453–470.

Bajoghli, Narges. 2019. *Iran Reframed: Anxieties of Power in the Islamic Republic*. Palo Alto, CA: Stanford University Press.

Bakalian, Anny, and Mehdi Bozorgmehr. 2005. "Muslim American Mobilization." *Diaspora: A Journal of Transnational Studies* 14: 7–43.

Barker, Martin. 1981. *New Racism: Conservatives and the Ideology of the Tribe.* London: Junction Books.

Barot, R., and J. Bird. 2001. "Racialization: The Genealogy and a Critique of a Concept." *Ethnic and Racial Studies* 24 (4): 601–618.

Bayoumi, Moustafa. 2009. *How Does It Feel to Be a Problem? Being Young and Arab in America.* London: Penguin Books.

BBC News. 2010. "UN Sanctions against Iran." July 26. www.bbc.com.

———. 2019a. "Europe and Right-Wing Nationalism: A Country-by-Country Guide." November 13. www.bbc.com.

———. 2019b. "Six Charts That Show How Hard US Sanctions Have Hit Iran." December 9. www.bbc.com.

Behdad, Ali. 2005. *A Forgetfulness Nation: On Immigration and Cultural Identity in the United States.* Durham, NC: Duke University Press.

Benaquisto, L. 2008. "Codes and Coding." In *The SAGE Encyclopedia of Qualitative Research Methods,* edited by Lisa M. Given. Thousand Oaks, CA: Sage.

Blake, John. 2010. "Arab- and Persian-American Campaign: 'Check It Right' on Census." CNN. May 14. www.cnn.com.

Bloemraad, Irene. 2006. *Becoming a Citizen: Incorporating Immigrants and Refugees in the United States and Canada.* Berkeley: University of California Press.

Bonilla-Silva, Eduardo. 1997. "Rethinking Racism: Towards a Structural Interpretation." *American Sociological Review* 62: 465–480.

———. 2000. "This Is a White Country: The Racial Ideology of the Western Nations of the World System." *Sociological Inquiry* 70 (2): 188–214.

———. 2004. "From Bi-racial to Tri-racial: Towards a New System of Racial Stratification in the USA." *Ethnic and Racial Studies* 27 (6): 931–950.

———. 2017. *Racism without Racists: Color-Blind Racism and the Persistence of Racial Inequality in the US,* 5th ed. Lanham, MD: Rowman & Littlefield.

Bonilla-Silva, Eduardo, and Sarah Mayorga. 2011. "On (Not) Belonging: Why Citizenship Does Not Remedy Racial Inequality." In *State of White Supremacy: Racism, Governance, and the United States,* edited by Moon-Kie Jung, Joao H. Costa Vargas, and Eduardo Bonilla-Silva. Palo Alto, CA: Stanford University Press.

Bosniak, Linda. 2000. "Citizenship Denationalized." *Journal of Global Legal Studies* 7 (2): 456–488.

Bozorgmehr, Mehdi. 1998. "From Iranian Studies to Studies of Iranians in the United States." *Iranian Studies* 31: 5–30.

———. 2000. "Does Host Hostility Create Ethnic Solidarity? The Experience of Iranians in the U.S." *Bulletin of the Royal Institute for Inter-Faith Studies* 2 (1): 159–178.

———. 2007. "Iran." In *The New Americans: A Guide to Immigration since 1965,* edited by Mary C. Waters and Reed Ueda. Cambridge, MA: Harvard University Press.

Bozorgmehr, Mehdi, and Daniel Douglas. 2011. "Success(ion): Second-Generation Iranian Americans." *Iranian Studies* 44: 3–24.

Bozorgmehr, Mehdi, and Georges Sabbagh. 1988. "High Status Immigrants: A Statistical Profile of Iranians in the US." *Iranian Studies* 21: 33–34.

Brubaker, Rogers. 1992. *Citizenship and Nationhood in France and Germany.* Cambridge, MA: Harvard University Press.

Bruner, Lane. 2011. "Rhetorical Studies and National Identity Construction." *National Identities* 13 (4): 403–414.

Byng, Michelle. 2008. "Complex Inequalities: The Case of Muslim Americans after 9/11." *American Behavioral Scientist* 51 (5): 659–674.

Cainkar, Louise. 2006. "The Social Construction of Difference and the Arab American Experience." *Journal of American Ethnic History* 25 (2/3): 243–278.

———. 2009. *Homeland Insecurity: The Arab American and Muslim American Experience after 9/11.* New York: Russell Sage.

Cainkar, Louise, and Saher Selod. 2018. "Review of Race Scholarship and the War on Terror." *Sociology of Race and Ethnicity* 4 (2): 165–177.

Carrera, Sergio. 2006. "A Comparison of Integration Programmes in the EU, Trends and Weaknesses." CEPS Challenge Paper No. 1. March 1. www.ceps.eu.

Center for Constitutional Rights. 2019. "The Muslim Ban: Discriminatory Impacts and Lack of Accountability." January 14, https://ccrjustice.org.

Chaichian, Mohammad. 1997. "First-Generation Iranian Immigrants and the Question of Cultural Identity: The Case of Iowa." *International Migration Review* 31 (3): 612–627.

Chappell, Bill. 2019. "U.S. Labels Iran's Revolutionary Guard as a Terrorist Organization." NPR. April 8. www.npr.org.

Chehabi, H. E. 2012. "Goethe Institute." Iranica Online. https://iranicaonline.org.

Clarkson, Alexander. 2013. *Fragmented Fatherland: Immigration and Cold War Conflict in the Federal Republic of Germany, 1945–1980.* New York: Berghahn Books.

Clayton, Jonathan, and Hereward Holland. 2015. "Over One Million Sea Arrivals Reach Europe in 2015." United Nations Refugee Agency (UNHCR). www.unhcr.org.

Collins, Patricia Hill. 1999. *Black Feminist Thought: Knowledge, Consciousness, and the Politics of Empowerment*, 2nd ed. New York: Routledge.

Crul, Maurice, and Jeroen Doomernik. 2003. "The Turkish and Moroccan Second Generation in the Netherlands: Divergent Trends between and Polarization within the Two Groups." *International Migration Review* 37 (4): 1039–1064.

Crul, Maurice, and Jens Schneider. 2009. "Comparative Integration Context Theory: Participation and Belonging in New Diverse European Cities." *Ethnic and Racial Studies* 33 (7): 1249–1268.

Crul, Maurice, and Hans Vermeulen. 2003. "The Second Generation in Europe." *International Migration Review* 37 (4): 965–986.

Dabashi, Hamid. 2007. *Iran: A People Interrupted.* New York: New Press

———. 2012. "War by Other Means." Al Jazeera News. June 27. www.aljazeera.com.

Daha, Maryam. 2011. "Contextual Factors Contributing to Ethnic Identity Development of Second-Generation Iranian American Adolescents." *Journal of Adolescent Research* 26: 543–569.

Dallalfar, Arlene. 1994. "Iranian Women as Immigrant Entrepreneurs." *Gender and Society* 8 (4): 541–561.

Darvishpour, Mehrdad. 2002. "Immigrant Women Challenge the Role of Men: How the Changing Power Relationship within Iranian Families in Sweden Intensifies Family Conflicts after Immigration." *Journal of Comparative Family Studies* 33: 271–296.

Davar, Faramarz. 2020. "The Diplomat King: The Shah's Foreign Policy." IranWire. July 27. https://iranwire.com.

Davila, Arlene. 2008. *Latino Spin: Public Image and the Whitewashing of Race*. New York: NYU Press.

Davis, Angela Y. 1981. *Women, Race, and Class*. New York: Random House.

Degler, Eva, and Thomas Liebig. 2017. "Finding their Way: Labour Market Integration of Refugees in Germany." OECD. www.oecd.org.

Delcker, Janosch. 2016. "The Phrase That Haunts Angela Merkel." Politico. August 19. www.politico.eu.

Denzin, N. K. 1991. "Representing Lived Experience in Ethnographic Texts." In *Studies in Symbolic Interaction*, vol. 12. Greenwich, CT: JAI Press.

Denzin, N. K., and Y. S. Lincoln, eds. 2000. *Handbook of Qualitative Research*, 2nd ed. Thousand Oaks, CA: Sage.

———. 2005. *Handbook of Qualitative Research*, 3rd ed. Thousand Oaks, CA: Sage.

Der-Martirosian, Claudia. 2008. *Iranian Immigrants in Los Angeles: The Role of Networks and Economic Integration*. New York: LFB Scholarly Publishing.

Deutsche Welle. 2009a. "German Interior Minister Pledges to Improve Turkish Integration." January 2. www.dw.com.

———. 2009b. "Study Shows Turkish Immigrants Least Integrated in Germany." January 26. www.dw.com.

———. 2016. "Study: Muslim Women Face Discrimination in German Job Market." September 20. www.dw.com.

———. 2019. "Germany: Number of Right-Wing Extremists Rose by a Third in 2019." December 16. www.dw.com.

DeLuce, Dan. 2022. "Trump's 'Poison Pill' Threatens Revival of Iran Nuclear Deal." NBC News. April 16. www.nbcnews.com.

Destatis (Statistisches Bundesamt). 2011. *Zensus: Population with a Migrant Background*. www.destatis.de.

Destatis (Statistisches Bundesamt). 2015. *Persons of a Migrant Background, Methodological Notes*. www.destatis.de.

DeYoung, Karen. 2022. "Experts Urge Return to Iran Nuclear Deal as Prospects Grow Dim." *Washington Post*. April 21. www.washingtonpost.com.

Du Bois, William Edward Burghardt. 1984 [1940]. *Dusk of Dawn: An Essay toward an Autobiography of a Race Concept*. Piscataway, NJ: Transaction Publishers.

El-Tayeb, Fatima. 1999. "Blood Is a Very Special Juice." *International Review of Social History* 44: 149–169.

European Union Center of North Carolina. 2008. "Europe's Iran Diplomacy." EU Briefings. March. https://europe.unc.edu.

Fatemi, Khosrow. 1980. "The Iranian Revolution: Its Impact on Economic Relations with the United States." *International Journal of Middle East Studies* 12 (3): 303–317.

Fredrickson, George M. 2002. *Racism: A Short History*. Princeton, NJ: Princeton University Press.

Gesley, Jenny. 2017. "Germany: The Development of Migration and Citizenship Law in Postwar Germany." Law Library of Congress. March. www.loc.gov.

Ghorashi, Halleh. 1997. "Shifting and Conflicting Identities: Iranian Women Political Activists in Exile." *European Journal of Women's Studies* 4: 283–303.

Gladstone, Rick. 2018. "Trump Travel Ban: How It Affects the Countries." *New York Times*. June 26. www.nytimes.com.

Glenn, Evelyn Nakano. 2002. *Unequal Freedom: How Race and Gender Shaped American Citizenship and Labor*. Cambridge, MA: Harvard University Press.

Golash-Boza, Tanya, and William Darity, Jr. 2008. "Latino Racial Choices: The Effects of Skin Colour and Discrimination on Latinos' and Latinas' Racial Self-Identifications." *Ethnic and Racial Studies* 31 (5): 899–934.

Goldberg, A., D. Mourinho, and U. Kulke. 1996. "Labor Market Discrimination against Foreign Workers in Germany." *International Migration Papers*, 7.

Goldberg, David Theo. 2008. *The Threat of Race: Reflections on Racial Neoliberalism*. Malden, MA: Blackwell.

Gontanda, Neil. 2011. "The Racialization of Islam in American Law." *Annals of the American Academy of Political and Social Science* 637 (1): 184–195.

Gordon, Joy. 2013. "The Human Costs of the Iran Sanctions." *Foreign Policy*. October 18. https://foreignpolicy.com.

Gordon, Milton. 1964. *Assimilation in American Life: The Role of Race, Religion, and National Origins*. New York: Oxford University Press.

Green, Simon. 2000. "Beyond Ethnoculturalism? German Citizenship in the New Millennium." *German Politics* 9 (3): 105–124.

———. 2001a. "The Greens and the Reform of Citizenship Law." *ECPR Joint Session*.

———. 2001b. "Immigration, Asylum and Citizenship in Germany: The Impact of Unification and the Berlin Republic." *West European Politics* 24 (4): 82–104.

Grosfoguel, Ramón. 1997. "Colonial Caribbean Migrations to France, the Netherlands, Great Britain, and the United States." *Ethnic and Racial Studies* 20 (3): 594–612.

Gualtieri, Sarah. 2001. "Becoming 'White': Race, Religion, and the Foundations of Syrian/Lebanese Ethnicity in the United States." *Journal of American Ethnic History* 20 (4): 29–58.

Gubrium, Jaber F., and James A. Holstein. 1997. *The New Language of Qualitative Method*. Oxford: Blackwell.

Haasler, Simone. 2020. "The German System of Vocational Education and Training: Challenges of Gender, Academisation and the Integration of Low-Achieving Youth." *European Review of Labour and Research* 26 (1): 57–71.

Haddad, Yvonne. 2000. "The Dynamics of Islamic Identity in North America." In *Muslims on the Americanization Path*, edited by Yvonne Haddad and John Esposito. Oxford: Oxford University Press.

Hakimzadeh, Shirin. 2006. "Iran: A Vast Diaspora Abroad and Millions of Refugees." Migration Policy Institute. September 1. www.migrationpolicy.org.

Harding, Sandra. 2004. *The Feminist Standpoint Theory Reader: Intellectual and Political Controversies*. New York: Routledge.

hooks, bell. 1981. *Ain't I a Woman? Black Women and Feminism*. Boston: South End Press.

Hosseini-Kaladjahi, Hassan. 1997. *Iranians in Sweden: Economic, Cultural and Social Integration*. Stockholm: Almqvist & Wiksell International.

Howard, Marc Morje. 2008. "The Causes and Consequences of Germany's New Citizenship Law." *German Politics* 17 (1): 41–62.

Husain, Atiya. 2017. "Retrieving the Religion in Racialization: A Critical Review." *Sociology Compass* 11 (9).

Hussain, Murtaza. 2021. "The Iran War That Obama Tried to Avoid Is Now Around the Corner." Intercept. December 7. https://theintercept.com.

Jawad, Haifaa. 2003. "Historical and Contemporary Perspectives of Muslim Women Living in the West." In *Muslim Women in the United Kingdom and Beyond*, edited by Haifaa Jawad and Tansin Benn. Boston: Brill.

Johnson, John. 2001. "In-Depth Interviewing." *Handbook of Interview Research: Context and Method*, edited by James A. Holstein and Jaber F. Gubrium. Thousand Oaks, CA: Sage.

Joppke, Christian. 1999. *Immigration and the Nation-State: The United States, Germany, and Great Britain*. Oxford: Oxford University Press.

Kasinitz, Philip, John H. Mollenkopf, Mary C. Waters, and Jennifer Holdaway. *Inheriting the City: The Children of Immigrants Come of Age*. Cambridge, MA: Harvard University Press.

Kerber, Linda. 1997. "The Meanings of Citizenship." *Journal of American History* 84 (3): 833–854.

Khaled, Fatma. 2020. "Data: Iranians Affected the Most by Trump's Ban." Documented. October 13. https://documentedny.com.

Khatib-Shahidi, Rashid Armin. 2013. *German Foreign Policy towards Iran before World War II: Political Relations, Economic Influence, and the National Bank of Persia*. London and New York: I.B. Tauris.

Khosravi, Shahram. 1999. "Displacement and Entrepreneurship: Iranian Small Businesses in Stockholm." *Journal of Ethnic and Migration Studies* 25 (3): 493–508.

Kohn, Hans. 1957. *American Nationalism: An Interpretative Essay*. New York: Macmillan.

Kozhanov, Nikolay A. 2011. "U.S. Economic Sanctions against Iran: Undermined by External Factors." *Middle East Policy* 18 (3): 144–160.

Kurthen, Hermann. 1995. "Germany at the Crossroads: National Identity and the Challenges of Immigration." *International Migration Review* 29 (4): 914–938.

Lamont, Michele, Stefan Beljean, and Matthew Clair. 2014. "What Is Missing? Cultural Processes and Causal Pathways to Inequality." *Socio-Economic Review* 12 (3): 573–608.

Lamont, Michelle, and Virag Molinar. 2002. "The Study of Social Boundaries in the Social Sciences." *Annual Review of Sociology* 28: 167–195.

Leise, Eric. 2007. "Germany Strives to Integrate Immigrants with New Policies." Migration Policy Institute. July 9. www.migrationpolicy.org.

Levitt, Peggy, and Nina G. Schiller. 2004. "Conceptualizing Simultaneity: A Transnational Social Field Perspective on Society." *International Migration Review* 38 (3): 1002–1039.

Lewin, Fereshteh Ahmadi. 2001. "Identity Crisis and Integration: The Divergent Attitudes of Iranian Immigrant Men and Women towards Integration into Swedish Society." *International Migration* 39: 121–135.

Lindert, Annet, Hubert Korzilius, Fons Vijver, Sjaak Kroon, and Judit Arends-Toth. 2008. "Perceived Discrimination and Acculturation among Iranian Refugees in the Netherlands." *International Journal of Intercultural Relations* 32: 578–588.

Lofland, John, and Lyn H. Lofland. 1995. *Analyzing Social Settings*, 3rd ed. Belmont, CA: Wadsworth.

Maghbouleh, Neda. 2017. *The Limits of Whiteness: Iranian Americans and the Everyday Politics of Race*. Stanford, CA: Stanford University Press.

Mahdavi, Sara. 2006. "Held Hostage: Identity Citizenship of Iranian Americans." *Texas Journal on Civil Liberties and Civil Rights* 11 (2): 211–244.

Maira, Sunaina. 2009. *Missing: Youth, Citizenship, and Empire after 9/11*. Durham, NC: Duke University Press.

Majaj, Lisa Suheir. 2000. "Arab Americans and the Meanings of Race." In *Postcolonial Theory and the United States: Race, Ethnicity and the Literature*, edited by Amritjit Singh and Peter Schmidt. Jackson: University Press of Mississippi.

Malek, Amy. 2019. "The Paradoxes of Dual Nationality: Geopolitical Constraints on Multiple Citizenship in the Iranian Diaspora." *Middle East Journal* 73 (4): 531–554.

Marvasti, Amir, and Karyn McKinney. 2004. *Middle Eastern Lives in America*. Lanham, MD: Rowman & Littlefield.

McAuliffe, Cameron. 2007. "Visible Minorities: Constructing and Deconstructing the 'Muslim Iranian' Diaspora." In *Geographies of Muslim Identities: Diaspora, Gender, and Belonging*, edited by Cara Aitchison, Peter Hopkins, and Mei-Po Kwan. Burlington, VT: Ashgate.

Menashri, David. 1992. *Education and the Making of Modern Iran*. Ithaca, NY: Cornell University Press.

Messner, Michael. 2012. "Boyhood, Organized Sports, and the Construction of Masculinities." In *Readings for Sociology*, 7th ed., edited by Garth Massey. New York: W.W. Norton.

Miles, Robert. 1989. *Racism*. Routledge: London.

Miller, Lin. 2003. "Belonging to Country: A Philosophical Anthropology." *Journal of Australian Studies* 27 (76): 215–223.

Mills, Charles. 1997. *The Racial Contract*. Ithaca, NY: Cornell University Press.

Min, Pyong Gap, and Mehdi Bozorgmehr. 2000. "Immigrant Entrepreneurship and Business Patterns: A Comparison of Koreans and Iranians in Los Angeles." *International Migration Review* 34: 707–738.

Mirsepassi, Ali. 2000. *Intellectual Discourse and the Politics of Modernization. Negotiating Modernity in Iran*. New York: Cambridge University Press.

Mitchell, Christopher. 1989. "International Migration, International Relations and Foreign Policy." *International Migration Review* 23 (3): 681–708.

Moallem, Minoo. 2003. "Transnationalism and Immigrant Entrepreneurship: Iranian Diasporic Narratives from the United States, France, England, and Germany." In *The Social Construction of Diversity*, edited by Christiane Harzig and Danielle Juteau. New York: Berghahn Books.

Mobasher, Mohsen. 2012. *Iranians in Texas: Migration, Politics, and Ethnic Identity*. Austin: University of Texas Press.

Modarres, Ali. 1998. "Settlement Patterns of Iranians in the United States." *Iranian Studies* 31 (1): 31–49.

Mostashari, Ali, and Ali Khodamhosseini. 2004. "An Overview of Socioeconomic Characteristics of the Iranian-American Community Based on the 2000 U.S. Census." Iranian Studies Group at MIT. February. www.isgmit.org.

Mostofi, Nilou. 2003. "Who We Are: The Perplexity of Iranian-American Identity." *Sociological Quarterly* 44 (4): 681–703.

Mueller, A. Ulrike. 2012. "Far Away So Close: Race, Whiteness, and German Identity." *Identities: Global Studies in Culture and Power* 18 (6): 620–645.

Muller, Claus. 2006. "Integrating Turkish Communities: A German Dilemma." *Population Research Policy Review* 25 (5/6): 419–441.

Naber, Nadine. 2008. "Arab Americans and U.S. Racial Formations." In *Race and Arab Americans before and after 9/11: From Invisible Citizens to Visible Subjects*, edited by Amaney Jamal and Nadine Naber. Syracuse, NY: Syracuse University Press.

Naficy, Hamid. 2012. *A Social History of Iranian Cinema, Volume 4: The Globalizing Era, 1984–2010*. Durham, NC: Duke University Press.

NIAC. 2010. "NIAC Works to Prevent Banking Sanctions from Hitting Innocent Iranian Americans." National Iranian American Council Report. October 8. www.niacouncil.org.

Noack, Rick, and Rachel Pannett. 2021. "Far-Right French Presidential Candidate Put in Headlock by Protester at Rally." *Washington Post*. December 6. www.washingtonpost.com.

O'Connor, Tom. 2018. "Do US Sanctions Hurt Iran? Yes, and It's Everyday People That Suffer Most." *Newsweek*. November 15. www.newsweek.com.

OECD. 2013. *Stocks and Flows of Immigrants, 2003–2013*. www.oecd.org.

Oezcan, Veysel. 2004. "Germany: Immigration in Transition." Migration Policy Institute. July 1. www.migrationpolicy.org.

Omi, Michael, and Howard Winant. 1986. *Racial Formation in the United States: From the 1960s to the 1980s*. London: Routledge.

Ostrand, Nicole. 2015. "The Syrian Refugee Crisis: A Comparison of Responses by Germany, Sweden, the United Kingdom, and the United States." *Journal on Migration and Human Security* 3 (3): 255–279.

Ozkirimli, Umut. 2010. *Theories of Nationalism: A Critical Introduction*, 2nd ed. New York: Palgrave Macmillan.

Paone, Anthony, and Thomas Leigh. 2021. "Far-Right French Presidential Hopeful Promises 'Reconquest' at Rally." Reuters. December 6. www.reuters.com.

Park, Robert, and Ernest Burgess. 1969 [1921]. "Assimilation." In *Introduction to the Science of Sociology*. Chicago: University of Chicago Press.

Parsi, Trita. 2019. "Trump's 'Genocidal' Tweets against Iran Come with a Price." Truthout. May 21. https://truthout.org.

Parvini, Sarah, and Ellis Simani. 2019. "Are Arabs and Iranians White? Census Says Yes, but Many Disagree." *Los Angeles Times*. March 28. www.latimes.com.

Perea, Juan F. 1998. "Am I an American or Not? Reflections on Citizenship, Americanization, and Race." In *Immigration and Citizenship in the 21st Century*, edited by Noah Pickus. Lanham, MD: Rowman & Littlefield.

Perez, Lisandro. 2007. "Cuba." In *The New Americans: A Guide to Immigration since 1965*, edited by Mary C. Waters and Reed Ueda. Cambridge, MA: Harvard University Press.

Portes, Alejandro, and Robert D. Manning. 1986. "The Immigrant Ethnic Enclave: Theory and Empirical Examples." In *Competitive Ethnic Relations*, edited by Susan Olzak and Joane Nagel. Orlando, FL: Academic Press.

Portes, Alejandro, and Rubén G. Rumbaut. 1990. *Immigrant America: A Portrait*. Berkeley: University of California Press.

———. 2001. *Legacies: The Story of the Immigrant Second Generation*. Berkeley: University of California Press.

Rana, Junaid. 2011. *Terrifying Muslims: Race and Labor in the South Asian Diaspora*. Durham, NC: Duke University Press.

Rezaian, Jason. 2018. "Call Trump's Ban What It Is: An Iran Ban." *Washington Post*. June 26. www.washingtonpost.com.

Richards, David A. J. 1999. *Italian-American: The Racializing of an Ethnic Identity*. New York: NYU Press.

Ross, Dennis. 2021. "The Threat of War Is the Only Way to Achieve Peace with Iran." *Foreign Policy*. October 27. https://foreignpolicy.com.

Sadeghi, Sahar. 2016. "The Burden of Geopolitical Stigma: Iranian Immigrants and Their Adult Children in the US." *Journal of International Migration and Integration* 17: 1109–1124.

———. 2018a. "Host Discrimination, Bounded Belonging, Bounded Mobility: Experiences of Iranian Immigrants in Germany." In *The Iranian Diaspora: Challenges,*

Negotiations, and Transformations, edited by Mohsen Mostafavi Mobasher. Austin: University of Texas Press.

———. 2018b. "Racial-Ethnic Boundaries, Stigma, and the Re-emergence of 'Always Being Foreigners': Iranians and the Refugee Crisis in Germany." *Ethnic and Racial Studies* 42 (10): 1613–1631.

Safi, Mirna. 2010. "Immigrants' Life Satisfaction and in Europe: Between Assimilation and Discrimination." *European Sociological Review* 2: 159–176.

Said, Edward. 1978. *Orientalism*. New York: Vintage.

———. 1981. *Covering Islam: How the Media and Experts Determine How We See the Rest of the World*. New York: Vintage.

Sanchez, Tatiana. 2019. "Families Separated by Trump Travel Ban Sue over Waiver Delays." *San Francisco Chronicle*. November 9. www.sfchronicle.com.

Selod, Saher. 2015. "Citizenship Denied: The Racialization of Muslim Men and Women Post-9/11." *Critical Sociology* 41(1): 77–95.

Setayesh, Sogol, and Tim K. Mackey. 2016. "Addressing the Impact of Economic Sanctions on Iranian Drug Shortages in the Joint Comprehensive Plan of Action: Promoting Access to Medicines and Health Diplomacy." *Globalization and Health* 12 (31).

Shannon, Matthew K. 2015. "American-Iranian Alliances: International Education, Modernization, and Human Rights during the Pahlavi Era." *Diplomatic History*, 39 (4): 661–668.

Shear, Michael D., Helene Cooper, and Eric Schmitt. 2019. "Trump Says He Was 'Cocked and Loaded' to Strike Iran, but Pulled Back." *New York Times*. June 21. www.nytimes.com.

Shotter, John. 1993. *Cultural Politics of Everyday Life: Social Constructionism, Rhetoric, and Knowing of the Third Kind*. Milton Keynes: Open University Press.

Silverstein, Paul. 2005. "Immigrant Racialization and the New Savage Slot: Race, Migration, and Immigration in the New Europe." *Annual Review of Anthropology* 34: 363–84.

Simon, Patrick. 2003. "France and the Unknown Second Generation: Preliminary Results on Social Mobility." *International Migration Review* 37 (4): 1091–1119.

Steinberg, Stephen. 2001. *Ethnic Myth: Race, Ethnicity, and Class in America*. Boston: Beacon Press.

Syed, Maleeha. 2019. "Behind the Manifesto: What Does the Patriot Front Actually Believe?" *Burlington Free Press*. September 18.

Tarock, Adam. 1996. "US-Iran Relations: Heading for Confrontation?" *Third World Quarterly* 17 (1): 149–167.

———. 2006. "Iran's Nuclear Programme and the West." *Third World Quarterly* 27 (4): 645–664.

Tehranian, John. 2007. "Selective Racialization: Middle-Eastern American Identity and the Faustian Pact with Whiteness." *Connecticut Law Review* 40 (4): 2–33.

———. 2009. *Whitewashed: America's Invisible Middle Eastern Minority*. New York: NYU Press.

Thomson, Mark, and Maurice Crul. 2007. "The Second Generation in Europe and the United States: How Is the Transatlantic Debate Relevant for Further Research on the European Second Generation?" *Journal of Ethnic Migration Studies* 33 (7): 1025–1041.

Tuan, Mia. 1998. *Forever Foreigners or Honorary Whites? The Asian Ethnic Experience.* New Brunswick, NJ: Rutgers University Press.

UNHCR (United Nations High Commissioner for Refugees). 2020. Refugee Data Finder. www.unhcr.org.

US Department of State. 2017. "Iran Sanctions" (archived content). https://2009-2017. state.gov.

Vasquez, Jessica M. 2010. "Blurred Borders for Some but Not 'Others.'" *Sociological Perspectives* 53 (1): 45–72.

Waldinger, Roger, and David Fitzgerald. 2004. "Transnationalism in Question." *American Journal of Sociology* 109 (5): 1177–1195.

Waters, Mary. 1990. *Ethnic Options: Choosing Identities in America.* Berkeley: University of California Press.

Weber, Beverly. 2016. "The German Refugee 'Crisis' after Cologne: The Race of Refugee Rights." *English Language Notes* 54 (2): 77–92.

Weichselbaumer, Doris. 2019. "Multiple Discrimination against Female Immigrants Wearing Headscarves." *ILR Review* 73 (3): 600–627.

Weiss, R. S. 1994. *Learning from Strangers: The Art and Method of Qualitative Interview Studies.* New York: Free Press.

Wimmer, Andreas. 2013. *Ethnic Boundary Making: Institutions, Power, Networks.* New York: Oxford University Press.

Worbs, Susanne. 2003. "The Second Generation in Germany: Between School and the Labor Market." *International Migration Review* 37 (4): 1011–1038.

Wright, Louisa. 2019. "US Denies German-Iranian Father Visa Needed to Attend Son's Funeral." Deutsche Welle. July 5. www.dw.com.

Zia-Ebrahimi, Reza. 2016. *The Emergence of Iranian Nationalism: Race and the Politics of Dislocation.* New York: Cambridge University Press.

Zimmerman, Nils. 2018. "German-Iranian Business Ties Growing Again." Deutsche Welle. January 2. www.dw.com.

Zolberg, Aristide R., and Long Litt Woon. 1999. "Why Islam Is like Spanish: Cultural Incorporation in Europe and the United States." *Politics & Society* 27 (1): 5–38.

Zucker, Norman. 1983. "Refugee Resettlement in the United States: Policy and Problems." *Annals of the American Academy of Political and Social Science* 467: 175–186.

INDEX

access/accessibility, 14, 59–60, 123, 147, 151–52, 176n3
adolescents, 3, 54–60, 61, 78–83, 182n17
advancement, 26–34; barriers to, 65, 100–105, 151. *See also* mobility
AfD. *See* Alternative for Germany
Afghanistan, 105–6, 137, 169
Africa, 10, 15, 38, 93–94, 105, 110, 124, 172n18
African Americans, 56, 91–92
agencies, college-placement, 28–29, 174n29
Ali (first-generational Iranian), 29–30, 174nn30–31
alienation, 112, 136–37
Alternative for Germany (AfD), 20, 88–89, 106–7, 118–19, 178n6, 183n5
aluminum production, 31, 174n32
ambiguity, racial, 12, 18, 41, 84–85, 123–27, 152
America. *See* United States (U.S.)
Anahita (second-generation Iranian), 102, 135–36
ancestry, 75–78, 87, 146–47; foreign, 89–93, 95, 99, 100–105, 109, 148; role in Germany of, 13–14, 18, 89–99, 102–5, 144–45, 148–52, 179n16
Anderson, Benedict, 171n7
Anna (second-generation Iranian), 98–99
anti-foreigner racism, German, 19–20, 87–91, 95–98, 100–105, 122, 132–33, 139, 146–49; following 2015 refugee crisis, 107–9, 112–16; following New Year's Eve 2015, 109–12
Anti-immigrant racism, 7, 66, 78–83, 140, 144, 164

anti-Iranian racism, US, 21, 35–41, 53–60, 66, 78–84, 175n40
anti-Middle Eastern racism, 4–5, 140
anti-Muslim racism, 7, 66, 77–83, 140, 144, 164
anxiety, 78–83, 85, 106, 118, 122, 154, 167–68
Arab-Israeli war, 15–16
Arab people, 4, 6, 15–16, 57, 110, 128, 132–33, 147, 172n10
Aref (second-generation Iranian), 64–65
Armenian Iranians, 164
Aryanism, 13, 99, 130–31
assimilation, 10, 180n23. *See also* integration (social/cultural)
asylum seekers/asylum policies, 6, 88, 175n48; in Germany, 4, 13, 39–46, 48, 89, 92, 101, 146; universal, 4, 22, 40, 42, 48. *See also* refugees
Ausländers (foreigners), 5–6, 88–99, 122, 149, 151, 155, 178n10
Austria, 45
aviation industry, 39
"Axis of Evil," 50, 60, 65, 84, 143
Azad (second-generation Iranian), 143

"bad foreigner" trope, 18–20, 119, 131–40, 151–53
Baker, Bobby B. (musician), 35
banks, 33, 64–65; German, 22–25; US, 25, 173n19
barriers to access/advancement, 17, 48–49, 65; in Germany, 7–8, 100–105, 117, 151–52, 155, 179n19. *See also* mobility
Behdad, Ali, 30
"being," 16, 141

197

ABOUT THE AUTHOR

SAHAR SADEGHI is Associate Professor of Sociology at Muhlenberg College, engaged in research on race, migration, global politics, and the Iranian diaspora.